Henry Scott Holland

On behalf of Belief

Sermons Preached in S. Paul's Cathedral. Second Edition

Henry Scott Holland

On behalf of Belief
Sermons Preached in S. Paul's Cathedral. Second Edition

ISBN/EAN: 9783337104696

Printed in Europe, USA, Canada, Australia, Japan

Cover: Foto ©Lupo / pixelio.de

More available books at **www.hansebooks.com**

ON BEHALF OF BELIEF

SERMONS

PREACHED IN S. PAUL'S CATHEDRAL

BY THE REV.
H. S. HOLLAND, M.A.

Canon and Precentor of S. Paul's

" O yet consider it again "

SECOND EDITION

LONDON
LONGMANS, GREEN, & CO.
AND NEW YORK: 15 EAST 16th STREET
1892

TO

THE VERY REVEREND

RICHARD W. CHURCH,

DEAN OF S. PAUL'S,

WHOSE NAME HAS EVER BEEN A SUCCOUR AND A JOY:

AND WHOM, NOW, IT IS MY HIGH AND HAPPY PRIVILEGE

TO BE PERMITTED

TO KNOW, TO SERVE, AND TO LOVE.

PREFACE

THE Apostles' Creed is mainly a plain statement of matters of fact; yet, as a formula of belief, it appeals, of course, *not* to the critical and calculative understanding which is used in the discussion or the examination of historical evidence, but to the spiritual and apprehensive faculties, which lay hold of eternal verities. It does so because the belief which it asks for is not the mere belief that the facts occurred. Such a belief would be quite possible, without anything that could be called "faith." What it asks for, as "faith," is the committal of the self to these facts as to spiritual acts, in which the eternal Love and Will of God have entered upon the scene of our human story, and have taken definite action therein. To these acts God stands committed. And to these acts He asks man to commit himself—to commit himself in his entire being, so that he may pass under their power and pressure, and accept all their consequences, and yield himself to that which God, in them, sets moving. So surrendering himself, he brings to bear upon himself the full force of those energies which the Eternal Love has evoked on his behalf.

This self-surrender to the power of the Divine action is "faith," and it is, therefore, an affair of the will, of love, of the spirit of dedication. No examination of historical evidence can produce it, or justify it, or explain it. All such discussion is below the mark; it cannot touch the secret springs; it cannot reach home to the vital matter.

This is why, in things of faith, a weariness, an insufficiency, belongs to all apologetic handling of historical evidence.

And, indeed, the believer cannot enter on such a discussion without a sincere and profound sense of apology for having to force into the foreground matter so inadequate. Yet his spiritual surrender of himself involves the facts being there: his faith rests absolutely on the assumption that God's Love has, as a fact, taken this action on his behalf. And, if this assumption is questioned, he is obliged to see to its justification.

It is to help towards this justification that I have ventured to print the first four sermons in this little book. They may possibly suggest to some the coherence of the entire Creed, which knits its ideal and its historical elements together into a unity so close and compact that it is impossible to effect a severance—impossible to separate, by any analysis, kernel from husk, where each element is kernel and husk by turns.

To these four sermons are added four others, which attempt to complete the pleas, already begun in another book, for that necessary and vital correspondence between faith and the Church, which is universally assumed in the apostolical writings.

The last four sermons endeavour to justify and interpret that loyalty to natural facts, which, far from being traversed, is rather sanctioned and confirmed by belief in a Risen Master, and in His Redemptive Church.

CONTENTS

Concerning the Resurrection.

PAGE

CRITICISM AND THE RESURRECTION 1
"*If Christ be not raised, your faith is vain.*"—
1 COR. xv. 17.

THE CRITICAL DILEMMA 25
"*If Christ be not raised, your faith is vain.*"—
1 COR. xv. 17.

THE GOSPEL WITNESS 50
"*Whereof we are all witnesses.*"—ACTS ii. 32.

THE ELEMENTAL ENIGMAS 77
"*We have seen and do testify that the Father sent the Son to be the Saviour of the world.*"—1 JOHN iv. 14.

Concerning the Church.

CORPORATE FAITH 102
"*Holding the Head, from which all the body by joints and bands having nourishment ministered, and knit together, increaseth with the increase of God.*"—
COL. ii. 19.

	PAGE
THE PATTERN IN THE MOUNT	123

"*After that He through the Holy Ghost had given commandments unto the Apostles whom He had chosen.*"
—ACTS i. 2.

OUR CITIZENSHIP 146

"*For the edifying of the Body of Christ.*"—EPH i. v. 12.

THE BUILDING OF THE SPIRIT 166

'*The Lord sitteth above the water-flood: and the Lord remaineth a King for ever.*"—PS. xxix. 10.

Concerning Human Nature.

"MADE UNDER THE LAW" 187

"*When the fulness of the time was come, God sent forth His Son, made of a woman, made under the law.*"—GAL. iv. 4.

THE DIVINE SANCTION TO NATURAL LAW 211

'*Therefore, O thou son of man, speak unto the house of Israel; Thus ye speak, saying, If our transgressions and our sins be upon us, and we pine away in them, how should we then live? Say unto them, As I live, saith the Lord God, I have no pleasure in the death of the wicked; but that the wicked turn from his way and live: turn ye, turn ye from your evil ways; for why will ye die, O house of Israel?*"—EZEK. xxxiii. 10, 11.

	PAGE
"The Word was made Flesh"	238

 "*And the Word was made flesh, and dwelt among us, and we beheld His glory, the glory as of the only-begotten of the Father.*"—John i. 14.

The Nature of the Flesh 262

 "*Hereby know ye the Spirit of God: Every spirit that confesseth that Jesus Christ is come in the flesh is of God.*"—1 John iv. 2.

CRITICISM AND THE RESURRECTION.

"If Christ be not raised, your faith is vain."—1 COR. xv. 17.

THE voice that speaks gives no uncertain sound. It is firm and vigorous enough. Here, certainly, is no shadowy outline, no vague emotion, no loose and unsteady outbreak of mystic rapture. The issue is stated in most sharp and decisive directness. No disguises, no veiling modifications, slip between. We still feel the shock of the startling frankness, of the unhesitating decision with which the voice rings out its terrible alternative: "If Christ be not raised, your faith is vain; ye are yet in your sins."

Yet it is the earliest voice with which we find Christianity speaking.

Let us remember where we are as we listen. We are back behind the written Gospels; earlier by some interval than the first three; earlier by thirty or forty years than the date at which tradition supposes the fourth to have been written. We are listening to the first voice with which historic Christianity speaks through recorded documents As soon as we find it at all, it is speaking in these decisive tones.

Nor are those tones, when you hear them, new S. Paul is appealing to a familiar truth, long held, long known to his hearers; appealing to it as the established fact on the strength of which they had been converted; appealing to it as to solid and undeniable ground, beyond all dispute or denial, on which he or they can take their stand in the new argument that has sprung up as to their own bodily resurrection. For already men were hotly discussing whether their own resurrection would be an actual, concrete, physical act in time, or an ideal, spiritual truth; so early, so rapidly were disputes at work which forced them to consider the value of facts. And it is in order to bring into the discussion some point of indisputable, unwavering certainty, wherewith to dispel the mists of a shifty, idealistic treatment, to touch solid ground, to have grip on something that could not fail, or totter, or crumble, or dissolve, that St. Paul takes his hearers back to the very ground of all belief, to the first premise of all discussion, to the core and heart of the Creed, "the Resurrection of Christ." Here, at any rate, he argues, is no idea, but a fact; no spiritual ideal, but an actual event. And just by the force of this, its concrete, solid, matter-of-fact actuality, it determined the question of their own resurrection in a sense directly contrary to that of the idealists.

"If Christ be not raised, your faith is vain." That earliest voice of the faith rings still in our ears, with its loud challenge to face, and measure, without flinching, the great issue that is ever before us. How sharply it pierces our souls, as we stand puzzled and distressed by all the sore anxieties which beset the discussions which have busied themselves with the origin of the Christian religion!

We have been flooded with new knowledge of

the old days in which S. Paul uttered this bold cry—new knowledge of the ways, and habits, and conditions of those earliest believers—ways and manners so strangely different from our own. We have gained knowledge, too, of a multitude of other religions, with their strange parallels to our own, yet with dissimilarities at least as strange. And, moreover, we have been given, too, not new knowledge only, but new methods of knowledge— methods, before unused, of comparison, of insight, of discovery, of judgment. And all these we cannot but bring to bear upon the matter of our belief; for we carry them with us, as we read the old books with minds already trained to appreciate the new materials and exercise the new methods.

Now, this being our case, it is of vital importance that we should make absolutely clear to ourselves what is the exact problem which the origin of the Christian religion offers to our critical examination. What is its distinctive characteristic?

It has, no doubt, many resemblances to the rise and movement of other religions; and these resemblances will permit of comparisons, and of speculative reconstructions, and of suggestive probabilities, by which we may pass across from the critical study of these other faiths to throw light on dark places in our Christian record.

But these cannot ever carry us, of course, to the heart of the problem ; for that must always lie, not in the resemblances, but in the differences.

The crucial task of all criticism is to fix on, to signalize, to detach, to notify, to examine that particular and unique point in a religious creed which marks it off from all other facts of the same general kind.

And this it will accomplish by searching for its main, and central, and peculiar thought. What, it will ask, is the idea which originates and animates this or that religion? What is the formation and conception at its root? What is it which accounts for its existence, and justifies its ardour, and prompts its primary activity, and moulds its growth, and directs its work, and distributes its limits and parts into their due place and proportion? What is that without which the religion under review is a mere medley of those spiritual elements which are the common matter of all religion? What is that by recognition of which all these common elements cease to be a chaos of possibilities, and come together into a distinct and forcible reality, rationally coherent, emphatically and vividly distinguishable from all other spiritual phenomena? On that point in each religion, whatever it be, criticism must relentlessly fasten; round and about that point it must loyally circle.

Now, there can be no doubt at all where the central, and originative, and distinctive point is to be discovered in the Christian religion. St. Paul has signalized it for us, once for all, in words that can never lose their tingling force of truth: "If Christ be not raised, your faith is vain; ye are yet in your sins."

Belief in the Resurrection is the root of Christianity. Everything runs back to it; everything flows from it.

For if there is any matter about which the Christian documents give authentic and unqualified evidence, it is to the absolute insufficiency of our Lord's earthly Life and Mission to give the momentum which originates a new religion. Nothing had been done at all, antecedent to the bitter end on Calvary, which can the least account for the after-consequences. Nothing stable had been rooted and established; nothing had taken more than the most tentative shape. There was no decisive and intelligible idea planted in the hearts of men with effective precision. Much had been dimly hinted; much seemed about to be happening. There was great talk of a kingdom that should come, of a Church that should be built. But nothing did come; nothing had happened; the kingdom did not appear; the Church was not built. Now and again the hopes of the crowd rose, and they cried aloud on some happy day, "Surely it has come! Is not this Messias? Was it ever seen in this fashion? We will make Him a king." And then He Himself deserted their hopes, defeated their longings, broke up their zeal. He fled; He hid; He scattered them. He set Himself to bewilder, to baffle, to disappoint them. Nothing came of it all, but a sense of splendid promise that yet never took shape or substance. No wonder that John the Baptist himself wondered at the fruitless postponement, and sent to inquire from the prison whether the kingdom was ever going to show itself.

And the few, the very few who clung in dumb loyalty to the Person Whose sublimity held them in thrall, they could not tell what it was that they had been called to receive, what thrones they were to occupy. They were lost in the enigmas offered them. Now they seemed to have got the thread of the Master's teaching; now it was lost. Whenever they thought that they understood, they found themselves the more perplexed. If they tried to make assertions of their own, they only blundered. Always, to the very last, they remained below the level of understanding demanded of them; without any fixed or intelligible creed to proclaim; possessed of nothing, that did not shatter into hopeless fragments under the shock of the naked Cross.

What a brief moment, after all, it had been! The broken bits of a couple of years were all that they had to look back upon; only a dozen or eighteen months of closer intercourse with the Master; and these months had been months not of gathering success or of steadying assurance, but months of failure, months of confusion, months of ever-darkening disaster,—months of flight or of desertion, of dreary pause, of disheartening suspense, of blind misunderstanding, of impenetrable mystery.

Once, and once only, had there looked like a gleam of daylight. Once, and once only, had there begun to be a moment at which the Master seemed to be preparing to act. Once, and once only, did He set Himself to own the Messiahship in a way that was comprehensible, and the dawn of the kingdom, so long deferred, seemed at last to draw near. It was that day for which He had prepared so carefully and so long, when He bade them bring the ass, and lay their garments upon it, and He rode as the prophetic King into Zion, and beneath Him were the strewn robes for royal feet, and about Him the waving palms of triumph, and before Him and behind Him the multitudes who shouted the Messianic greeting, "Hosanna in the highest." At last it was to begin; at last He would act. Ah! the despair! He takes but the first step, and, lo! it is His last. He makes but one challenge, and, lo! all is over. Down breaks the storm that had hung so long in black menace above Him. Down it sweeps—the roaring storm of hate, of cruelty, of rage. Down it sweeps, in one overpowering rush, and He is gone —gone! without a struggle, without an effort; gone! broken, defeated, crushed; not a shred remains of that fair promise; not a wreck is left behind of that shattered vision of hope and joy. All have forsaken and fled. No power breaks forth to shield Him; no refuge opens to Him a door of escape! His enemies have Him, hold Him, work their will on Him; they taunt Him for His impotence, without fear, without rebuke. Ah! well indeed if a horrible dread can be shut off from those stricken souls—a dread lest it is not only the work of man, but even the very curse of God Himself, that has fallen upon Him Who was hung on a tree!

Surely, in our love for the sweet memory of our Lord on earth, a Man among us so tender and so strong, we forget how it would have looked if nothing had ever followed; how terribly short and swift its passage; how miserably small and unstable its actual achievement! Nothing in that brief Life, taken by itself, can account for Christian belief in the Lord, or for the creation of the Church. It is the Resurrection which alone gave constructive force to the Life that lay behind it. A vision of unutterable beauty, indeed, that Life would ever have been; but a vision that came and passed and vanished before men's bewildered eyes had had time to secure it, or their hearts to apprehend what was there, for a fleeting moment, in their midst. A few deep, incomparable words would have lingered about their memories; a few marvellous hours would never be forgotten, in which the sick had known the touch of power, and the sorrow and sighing had all fled away. Some dozen men and a knot of women would have nursed a sick and fading secret, low buried in their silent souls—the secret of what once they had believed, as, in the tranced mystery of one historic evening, they had heard a quiet voice in their ears, which said, "Take, eat; this is My Body. Do this in memory of Me."

But the very memory of this high promise, of this passing vision, far from driving them forth on a victorious mission, could but break their hearts with despair, as they recalled the utter and absolute ruin in which it had been so swiftly engulfed!

In the Resurrection, it was not the Lord only Who was raised from the dead. His Life on earth rose with Him; it was lifted up into its real light. That which had been but a suggestion, but a fragment, but a disappointment, but a failure, won, for the first time, out of the Resurrection a force that gave it significance and cohesion. The Spirit had come upon it; and that which had been all partial and piecemeal now first cohered together and showed itself substantial, and became a living thing. Now, first, the promises gained reality, the vision became concrete, the symbolic acts obtained solid footing, the deep words lost their shadowy, intangible remoteness. A light flashed back from Easter morning, and poured daylight on what had been so dark. The events that had seemed so tangled and confusing now strung themselves together on a clear and comprehensible method. The cue was given, and all was intelligible.

We feel this in every word and motion of the Apostles. Every one knows, every one is astonished at, the entire change that has passed over them, between the Gospels and the earliest records stored for us in the Acts. The naturalness and yet the strangeness of this change is one of our most convincing evidences of the reliability of those primitive documents. The simplicity with which the transformation is told is overpoweringly persuasive. The men who, in the Gospels, never can win possession of the Lord's mind, never are level with His meaning, never can follow His transitions, never can ask a question without blundering, never can get sure of themselves, never can help misunderstanding His teaching, never can get out of themselves, never can understand to what the Master is leading them, not though He take them aside and prepare them, and shut Himself up with them to school them, and reiterates again and again the deliberate purpose with which He goes to Jerusalem; the men who were still, after all the miracles, without understanding—having ears, heard not; the men who understood none of those things, but the "saying was hid from them, and they perceived not the things that were said;" the men who could despair, as Thomas, or could forsake, as all did, or could deny, as Peter;—these very men are found, in the first chapter of the Acts, in complete and secure possession of the Lord's secret. Yet they are the same men, with the same characters. Who can mistake them? John, with the same impressive silence; Cephas, with the same impetuous speech. Not that they are not still liable to painful complexities and struggles in the working out of the details; but of one thing they can never doubt again—they can never doubt what the significance was of the days during which they had walked and talked with Jesus during His sojourn on earth. That, from beginning to end—from the baptism of John until the day of His taking up—has become a consistent, coherent, intelligible act, complete and whole in all its parts. All the words that ever fell from the Master's lips, —words which then baffled, startled, upset, distressed them—are now to them clear and limpid as the day. Every syllable carries its meaning with it. And His mind is laid open to them, and they apprehend it with easy freedom; and their faith in Him is no longer a blind, personal fascination—" Lord, to whom shall we go?" it is rational, articulate, and secure. It knows its grounds; it puts out its reasons; it handles its premises; it is in possession of itself; it is beyond the possibility of mistrust or of bewilderment. They speak with emphasis, these men who once babbled like children; they act with decision, these who once were so incapable of initiation.

It is the Resurrection that has made the change. The Resurrection is the core of truth, in which and to which all adheres. It is to them the animating, formative fact, which interprets, which justifies, which supports, which quickens the fabric of faith and life. They have got fast hold of the key; therefore every lock once closed flies open. They stand in the light, and therefore stumble no longer. The path is clear, the gate is open; they know the road they have to travel. "Lord," they had once cried in blank bewilderment, "we know not whither Thou goest, and how can we know the way?" Now they understand whither He has gone; and therefore He Who is the Resurrection is at once made to them also the Way, the Truth, and the Life.

What, then, are we to say of a school of criticism, with which we are all familiar, which finds a parallel to our Gospel in the stories of those heroes whose lives were so momentous and so masterful, that when they died no one could believe them to have passed away? So long and so deeply had they occupied the world's drama, that the stage seemed empty without their name to fill it; so that still men's eyes looked for some mysterious return of the vanished presence, and still their ears listened for some rallying cry from the voice that could not, surely, be lost for ever.

Such dim hopes, faintly lingering round the grave of some King Arthur, or some Frederic Barbarossa, or even round the close of some hideous nightmare, like the tyranny of Nero, embody and symbolize nothing else but the profound impression which their actual lives had built up and established, until it had become a part of the common material of general human existence. The violence of its swift removal leaves behind a vague pain, a hunger, a wonder; and these may relieve themselves in mythical expectations, in mysterious rumours, in haunting hopes, which gather like clouds at evening round a setting sun, and glow with ravishing splendour for some rare moments, before they pale and scatter under the chill wind of that night which is ever creeping up, ashen and relentless. So a "cloud of myth" may hang loose about the hero's vanishing; but the myth is meaningless and unintelligible, except as a reflex of the impressiveness and solidity and importance of the real life lived. It witnesses to that and to nothing else. Strip it away and the life remains, real, comprehensible, valid.

But what fragment of parallel is there here to the Gospel? With our Lord, it is not the *life* which makes the supernatural myth intelligible, but it is the supernatural act which alone makes the life intelligible. Here is no faint supernatural vapour, embosoming a solid core of impressive natural incidents. Nay! It is the human career which is so fragmentary, so slight, so rapid, so fleeting, until it is endowed with a solid core of substance and force by the marvel of the Resurrection. On that it stands; it is compacted by that; out from the Resurrection flows the energy which carries the entire story. It is by believing in His Resurrection that His followers first lay hold of the real significance of His Life on earth, and first acquire that vital faith in Him which constitutes them missionaries of a new religion.

This is the cardinal fact that has got to be accounted for; and any criticism, therefore—let us be sure of this—which fails to find the primary and original and formative germ of Christianity in the belief in a risen Lord; any criticism which supposes that this belief can be treated as surplusage, as a merely decorative accident, as the mythical expression of enthusiasm, as comparable to the apotheosis of a great heroic figure; any criticism which begins by omitting all this supernaturalism from its calculation, and sets itself to extract from the human story which preceded the death the motive impulse which explains the faith;—any such criticism as this, whatever form it take, has missed the point which it undertakes to explain. It has slipped off the scientific track; it has ruled itself out of court. Far from offering us a solution, it simply fails to meet the issue, for it omits the one essential and characteristic and vital element in the problem to be solved.

Beloved, we may discard such criticism from discussion, yet it remains that there are anxious and serious questions which beset and oppress us. Yes, indeed; and, before attempting to answer them, let us remember the one condition under which they can be met and solved. We shall only obtain certainty and conviction when the Resurrection has become to our own little human story on earth that which, in its unique degree, it was to the earthly Life of the Lord. It must become, I mean, the key which makes our own story intelligible, the cypher by which all its strange hieroglyphics can be read off and interpreted.

We who so sorely pine for certainty of intellectual conviction have to ask ourselves, first of all, whether we are living a life which demands our resurrection in Christ as its only adequate solution—a life which is built on that sure hope, formed after that pattern, sustained by that underlying motive; a life which schools itself after the discipline which such a hope imposes, curbing and bending the motives and the desires of the flesh so that they seek not here, in this fair but unstable earth, their home and their promise, but are ever forcing themselves into the strong current of the victorious will, which sets from within our deepest selves towards that far land of purity and peace to which He calls us, Who is the Living One, and was dead, and, behold, He is alive for evermore! Unless this be, in some measure, true, we could not know the certainty of Christ's Resurrection.

Let us ask ourselves, Would your ways and mine be incomprehensible if there were no Resurrection? Have we any motives, real and animating, on which we act, which would be meaningless if we were not to rise again? Have we made any moral venture on the strength of this assurance? Is there anything on earth that we could rightly have and hold, and yet which we deny ourselves, and treat as worthless, in face of the far more glorious hope set before us? Are we so living that we should be of all men most miserable, most silly, most befooled, if Christ be not raised?

Ah! surely, it is not only intellectually that the Resurrection is apt to seem to us but a piece of poetical supernaturalism, a decorative incident which satisfies the dramatic feelings, a relief to our artistic judgment, a beautiful picture at the end of an heroic life, an imaginative and visionary ideal. It too often is no more than this to our faith, as well as to our reason. It hangs loosely outside our own spiritual story. It lays no direct or forcible pressure upon our moral life. Yet, so long as this is so, we have not touched the core of the Christian verity. We have not reached its central secret, its heart of grace. Believe me, our faith is still vain if the Resurrection of Christ be not the fount and spring of all our living, the support on which we buttress ourselves, round which the very fibres of the practical will wind and bind themselves. Our faith is vain if the risen Christ be not the rock on which we rest, the refuge which we hide, the fortress out of which we descend to walk the lower ways of earth. Our faith is vain if the risen Christ be not the formative or energetic reality which dominates our mind, and regulates our practice, and shapes our thought, and controls our passions, and organizes our motives, and builds our character, and lays hands upon our entire self, to rule, possess, transform it. That is the "Christian life;" that is "walking in Christ." S. Paul can acknowledge nothing short of that.

Alas! it is because this resurrection life is so little true of us that our faith is so empty and vain. Alas! it is because this walking in the risen Christ is so strange to us, so unattempted, that we find ourselves lightly discussing the possibility of omitting the Resurrection from our Creed, and yet remaining as good Christians as we were before. God grant us grace, in fear and humiliation, to measure, by our readiness to imagine this possibility, the terrible interval which separates our practical daily religion from the faith of that Apostle who cried aloud to his trembling converts, "If Christ be not raised, your faith is vain; ye are yet in your sins."

THE CRITICAL DILEMMA.

"If Christ be not raised, your faith is vain."—1 COR. xv. 17.

HISTORICAL criticism is in the air. It is the force which stirs our brain into thinking. We are all under the sense of its quickening influence. And one of the tasks to which it invites us is that of disengaging the essence of our Christian religion from its accidents; of distinguishing the motive force which dictates the forward movement of the faith from all the incidental material which the central force puts to its own use and service. We are to free this, the solid kernel of original truth, from the husk in which the conditions of the century and the chances of the time have secreted it. Now, all our success, as we said, in such a search depends on our accurate and precise apprehension of what constitutes the actual root and heart of the Christian religion. And what this is, the religion itself alone can make evident. It is its own authority on such a matter. It alone can disclose, in its acknowledged creeds, through its recorded history, the secret of its vitality, the forces on which it relies, the powers and motives to which it makes its effective appeals. Historical criticism has got to discover, not what you or I may consider ought to have been the central assertion of Christianity, but simply what was it? What did it actually assume and prove to be its root-idea? By what proclamation did it win adherents? What was the essential core of its message to the world?

And if this is our task, it is strange indeed—as we have already tried to show—that we ever allow ourselves to imagine that this kernel would be found in the human career of Jesus of Nazareth, if only we could free it from its mythical and supernatural husk and allow it to terminate naturally with His heroic Death. Such a hope is bound to be fruitless, just because, if ever it could attain its end, if ever it could wring a consistent human story out of documents written expressly to convey the exactly opposite impression, then it must inevitably find that it had dropped, in the process, all the vital elements which constitute the force of the faith. For the supernatural resurrection, as we tried to show, is not one of a series of details the omission of which can be discussed as a practical possibility, as if it might be cut out, and yet the rest of the Creed remain what it was. For it is itself not a detail in the Creed, but the starting-point of the Creed itself. It is itself the substance of the revelation, the pregnant germ out of which the entire fabric of belief emerges, constructs itself, shapes its parts; without which it not only has no historical basis, but also has no intellectual principle of cohesion.

This is surely a most familiar truth; and yet, in view of the many earnest souls who still give themselves the profitless labour of this search after a purely natural basis for their belief in Jesus, it seems necessary to remind ourselves at length why it is so terribly true that "if Christ be not raised, our faith is vain." Let us note, therefore, the various ways in which the Resurrection thus creates the Creed.

The Resurrection, we said, gave the disciples the clue by which the fragmentary and abrupt life of our Lord was interpreted and justified. How, then, did it do this? What was the interpretation? First, it threw on it the light of prophecy. "He rose again the third day, according to the Scriptures." "According to the Scriptures." The entire body of ancient Scripture opened out its heart to the astonished and rejoicing Apostles. True, the early methods of exegesis are not ours, are very strange to us—present to us difficulties of their own. With this we have not to do now. But no strangeness of method can blind us to the fact that, in grasping the Resurrection, the Apostles had hold of a principle of interpretation which reconciled for them, and, under every variety of critical method, has reconciled ever since, the dilemma presented in prophecy by the double conception of a suffering and dying and yet victorious Messiah. The darkest passages of Isaiah and of the Psalms, speaking of a desolation, an agony, a death, which nevertheless issue in some strange outburst of triumphant exaltation—these passages, which had been the bewilderment of patient souls who had waited long for the redemption of Israel,—these were now become clear as the very day to the disciples. The paradox that once tormented was solved. God, then, was not, as those perplexing contrasts suggested, at cross-purposes with Himself; the promise of the Messiah was no black enigma, in which the visions traversed each other, and the voices broke off into harassing contradictions. Now they saw it to have had one unwavering purpose, which moved on to its fixed goal, unbroken by any counter-current. It was one Person Who drew every thread into the web of His own story. It was one manifestation which summed up all diversities of detail, which united, into one consistent act, elements most antithetical. The Scriptures, with all their fragments lying side by side, partial and unreconciled, come together bone to bone. " Oh, fools that they had been, and slow of heart to believe all that the prophets had spoken! Thus it was written: thus it behoved Christ to suffer, and to rise from the dead the third day!"

"It *behoved* Christ to suffer," if it behoved Him to rise again. Ah! here is a new point. Let us follow their argument out as they worked it

Christ's sufferings—Christ's death. These are no longer what they were. They had been in themselves the most miserable and the most signal victory that the power of evil had ever won. They had expressed and embodied the despair of good, trodden down in its blood under the tyrant heels of the oppressor. But, seen as leading on to the Resurrection, seen as involved in the Resurrection, they become wholly new things. A new level is taken, a fresh perspective. They are seen to belong to that high drama of salvation which God, through the long ages, had slowly been unrolling. God, in leading His Messiah down to the cross and the grave, was leading Him unto His victory. The Resurrection is God's justification of the Crucifixion.

It is His proof that all is well, that all on Calvary had a purpose in it. Easter does not repudiate Good Friday; rather, it reconciles Good Friday with that mind of God which was disclosed in the Resurrection. This is the strange news which all the old Scriptures had foreseen, and, by foreseeing had shown to be intentional and deliberate. "Christ must have suffered." "Suffering was the gate through which He ought to have entered into His glory." God, then, in all the misery, knew what He was doing. It was no terrible accident that brought the Messiah to His bloody end; no hideous nightmare in which the holiest life had been blindly trampled out, as by the brute hoofs of beasts. Nay, God's hand was on it; God's dominion never wavered; God's hold upon circumstance never slackened; God's scheme achieved itself in harmonious security, in perfect sequence. The hate, the malice, the cruelty, the sin, which had seemed to themselves to be so active in carrying out their own wicked counsels—they had never for a moment escaped the strong control of the Divine government; never, for one brief second, in their worst vehemence, ceased to grind, with their necks under His yoke, in the blessed service of His Will. "I wot, brethren, that through ignorance ye did it." "With wicked hands," indeed, they had done it; yet, for all their wickedness, they had but accomplished "the determinate counsel and foreknowledge of God."

Christ ought to have suffered; "it behoved;" it was right. All the Scriptures said it; and what they had said so long before must be part of a fixed design, of a scientific necessity, otherwise how could it be anticipated? And why? Why ought He to suffer? How could the Cross belong to the Divine plan? The moment they asked themselves this they knew the only possible answer. "Sacrifice," "Atonement," "Reconciliation by blood"—all the deep thoughts by which Christianity has shaken the world—these broke out upon the hearts of the Apostles, in a flash of magnificent insight, from the first moment in which the sun of Easter shot its rays back over Calvary. "It behoved Christ to have suffered!" It was a decree of God, a Divine necessity; and it was this because, as a Jew knew down to the very depth of his heart, sin could not cease but in sacrifice—because, without shedding of blood, there could be no remission of sins!

Oh, the daylight! Oh, the rapture of illumination! Oh, the mystery that throbbed in their enkindled souls and struggled for free loud utterance! "Oh, the depth of the riches, both of the wisdom and the knowledge of God! How unsearchable the judgments, and His ways past finding out!" The Resurrection has transformed the dark deed of Golgotha from a martyrdom into a sacrifice, from an heroic memory into a Divine and living atonement.

"Look back at the Cross," the Apostles cry. "What a transfiguration! That black, ungainly tree, so cruel, so hard, so blind, so terrible! Who could have believed the report? Unto whom was the arm of the Lord revealed? Ah, we ourselves, even we, had deemed Him stricken, smitten of God, afflicted, despised, rejected, from whom men hide their face! And, all the time, it was the Lord Whom it pleased to bruise Him. We see it now, clearly enough. The Lord declares it to us by raising Him from the dead. Jesus died for our sin by the same law by which He rose again for our justification. It was for our transgressions He was wounded, for our iniquities He was being bruised; it was the chastisement of our peace that was, at that awful hour, laid upon Him; and by those stripes, at which our sick memories shuddered with such speechless horror—lo! by those very stripes we were being healed."

Nor is it only backward that the Resurrection works. Not only does it give constructive force to the earthly life, and illuminative vitality to the ancient Scriptures, and transfiguring glory to the Cross: but it looks forward; it opens a way to new possibilities; it sets moving a wholly new world of thought, and power, and hope, and action; it uplifts the entire scene of human destinies to a fresh level of energy and gifts.

And it is here, above all, that we become conscious of the fallacy that was hidden in this foolish parallel between the belief in the Resurrection of the Lord and the fond myths and rumours that linger about a hero's grave. These are the last echoes of his loud activity, the closing glories that encircle and dignify his departure. But the essence of the Resurrection is that it is not the end, but the beginning. That which, in other stories, is the last flash of the dying sun, is here the first streak of the coming dawn. The activity of the Lord is in reserve, is withheld, until the Resurrection is past. His world-wide mission, His claim to the kingdom, His supremacy over sin, His paramount headship, His discharge of saving energy, His creation of the new manhood—these only become His by the resurrection from the dead, which declares Him then, first, to be the Son of God "with power."

"With power!" The supernatural story of the Resurrection and Ascension records, not His lingering departure, but His full arrival, in effectual strength, upon the drama of history. He goes, only in a way that gives Him power to come again, and to begin His great work, and establish His kingdom. So we are carried by the Resurrection to the grand beliefs which actually have built up His Church. We see why it was believed that the Sacrifice on the Cross abides, as an eternal fact, in His risen Body, offered and presented before God in high Heaven, where for ever He enters within the vail, bearing His blood; and for ever His blood intercedes, speaking better things than that of Abel, as it cries aloud for our forgiveness.

We see why the last memorial meal is endowed with an everlasting validity, rooted there, at the deepest heart of the Church, not as the sad shadow of a lost Presence remembered with tears, but as the " Eucharist," " the glad thanksgiving," the principal feast, the centre of all praise and song and adoration, the spring of unfailing joy, the living Bread, coming down for ever and ever from the eternal Heaven, that man may eat thereof and not die.

And again we see why, here on earth, there now rises, according to this belief, a fabric endowed with the strength of His risen Body, a CHURCH formed after the pattern of that Body now high in the Mount of God, and so becoming here, among men, that temple of His Body, which was to be raised again in three days, laid together, limb by limb, member by member, filling up the stature of His Body, holding fast by its risen Head, and growing with "the increase of God."

And all this is effected by that great Spirit Whom, by His Resurrection, He liberates — the Advocate, the Comforter; Whom He discharges from the Father—the Gift of all gifts, the Pledge of all certainty, all security, all peace.

But why go on? Why weary you? Surely it is plain enough, the moment we reflect at all, how it is that "if Christ be not raised, our faith is vain." For, clearly, these are the ideas, these are the forces, by which alone Christianity has, as a fact, won its way and conquered the world. These are the beliefs that have dictated all its preaching, have moulded its theology, have enthralled its hearers, have converted hearts, have framed the structure of its Church, have inspired its worship, have nerved its courage, have vitalized its hope, have given it "the victory that overcometh the world." Yet of all these beliefs the Resurrection is the core and kernel; without the Resurrection there is not one syllable of all this true. There is no pleading Cross; no blood of sprinkling; no prevailing intercession; no Church, which is the Body; no Eucharistic worship; no gift of the Comforter; no Christian walk in the newness of life.

Nor, again, is it only the mysteries of redemption and of worship that rest solely on the Resurrection as their key. We have but to recall the Epistles of S. Paul to see that every jot and tittle of Christian ethics begin and end in nothing but the Resurrection. The practical life of the believer is, for S. Paul, absolutely nothing else but this—the reproduction in one's self of the resurrection-life, of that eternal act in which Christ rose from the dead. He Who raised Jesus from the dead will work in us the same work, by the same mighty operation quickening our dead limbs into His righteousness, that, "like as Christ was raised from the dead through the glory of the Father, so we also might walk in newness of life." "Present yourselves, therefore, unto God, as alive from the dead, and your members as instruments of righteousness unto God." The ethical goal is simply to "attain, by any means, unto the resurrection from the dead."

And, moreover, see the pressing difficulty that meets us if we follow the criticism that hopes to find the kernel of Christianity in the human career stripped of its supernatural husk. The human Jesus, Whom we propose to discover, if He be what we are supposing, cannot have Himself initiated or originated any one of the main ideas, which are the root and strength of the Creed in His Name. He cannot have suggested Resurrection, or Atonement, or perpetual Intercession, or the sending of the Comforter. There is hardly a word of the early

Apostolic message to the world, recorded in the New Testament, which can owe anything to the man Jesus Who is preached. The conceptions which dominate all the thought, and construct all the language, and create all the appeals, and manipulate all the motives—these all take their first rise solely in the supernatural story, with which nevertheless the Master can have had nothing whatever to do. S. Paul must be the real originator of that Christ he preached—S. Paul, who, nevertheless, believed, with passionate fervour, that he and his own mind had ceased to exist or to act, since now it was not he that lived, but Christ Who lived in him.

Yes; it is the supernatural story which is, as a matter of fact, the only kernel of Christianity. This Idea of the Resurrection, of life out of death, of God come in the flesh, of atonement through blood, of the transfigured Intercessor, of the eternal Eucharist—this is the very core, the inspiration, the valid truth which has been won for man by Christ. This abides everlastingly verifiable—the key and standard of all human advance, of all spiritual purification.

And at this point a wholly different school of critics strikes in. It accepts the dilemma; it agrees eagerly with our argument. Our only mistake lies in supposing that this Idea, evoked into full life by the consciousness of S. Paul, must be encased in the miraculous story of a human career and death. This historical record is but the legendary wrapping by which the Idea appealed to the earlier imagination and emotion. But that is no longer needful, and, moreover, introduces the problem of the miraculous. It is now the task of the critical reason to strip off this mere garment of outward facts, which so picturesquely symbolize the purer truth. It is its office to prove the needlessness of this historical husk, to disengage from beneath the records the supreme spiritual essence in its veritable form. This is its task; and it is, therefore, wholly on the wrong tack when it devotes itself to desperate searches after an historical personage, and definite, consistent historical events, hidden behind the supernatural legend. Nay, it is just these historical events which it ought not to cling to, but to omit; for it is they that are the legend, while the idea which it is proposed to discard as legend is the only veritable and verifiable reality.

Now, those who so speak have this superiority over the rival school of criticism, in that they, at least, perceive where the core of our faith lies. They do not begin by omitting from their account all the main forces which initiated and impelled the Christian movement; they do not put themselves out of court by failing to face the problem, or to offer, at any rate, some solution of its difficulty. Christianity stands on the Resurrection; that they see well enough. Only, since miracles cannot happen, Christianity must stand, not on an historical event, but on a spiritual Idea.

Yes, these men see the point. And yet, if we face what is involved, with what a vigorous rebound our human instincts, our spiritual judgment, sweep back on the return wave of thought!

For do they mean, then, these men, that now, at this moment of our history, when every gathering motive, every motion of imagination, every effort of reason, are all bent on realizing the power of our common manhood, the significance of flesh and blood; now, when all of us are become so intensely alive to the touches of tender human nature, by which the whole world is made kin; now, when, under the pressure of this prevailing sympathy, all eyes and all hearts are turning, with a growing passion of attraction, towards that gracious human figure, which moves through the pages of those Gospel records—that sweet and masterful figure, so overwhelming in its simplicity, in its humanity, in its compassion, in its kindliness, in its patience, in its heroism, in its pathos; now, when, amid the drear and dragging years of man's painful history, all our keen researches, so damaging to a thousand reputations, have left to us but this one figure, which no scrutiny can impoverish and no discovery reduce—but this one figure on which we can endure to rest the eyes of our critical conscience with untainted reverence—but this one figure, before which we sink our voices and own the spell of some diviner secret than we can cover or account for, some secret of human dignity and peace that abides unflawed and unexampled;— do they mean that now, of all times, I am to be asked to surrender all this human story of Jesus of Nazareth as a child-fancy, which is immaterial to the idea it conveys—as a husk, which can be cast off as worthless now that the kernel is secured? What! to "know no more of Jesus after the flesh" —is that to mean that I am to remember no more Him Who sat on the hill and in the boat, and spake as man never spake; Him Who called to Him all the weary and heavy-laden; Him Whom all the sick and the suffering and the forlorn knew as their one Friend; Him Who drew to Him publican and harlot; Him Who had compassion for the widow in her tears, and for the crowd in their hunger; Him Who was pitiful to children, and took them in His arms, Who sat in the house at Bethany, and loved Mary, and Martha, and Lazarus;

Him Who forgave His murderers, and bade farewell to His Mother from the Cross, and won to Himself the heart of the dying thief; Him Who bowed His head under the olives, shaken by a passionate distress; Him Who, loving ever His own, loved them to the uttermost, and, even on the night He was betrayed, bade them remember Him always? Am I to surrender Him—to treat Him as needless? Ah, my God! is it my heart only that knows that that surrender can never be made? Is it not my thought, my reason, that protest with indignant refusal, knowing, with a certainty which nothing can ever dispute, that the Christian Idea is a mere lifeless ghost, impotent, and hollow, if there be once withdrawn from it the vital force which is given it by its identification with that warm, living, breathing humanity, which is Jesus of Nazareth, the Son of Mary, the Man of our flesh and of our blood, Who " was crucified, dead, and buried "?

How, then, shall we deal with the desperate situation? If, assuming that the Resurrection is impossible, we go with the one critical school, and cling to the mere human story, then we are driven to omit, as husk, all the ideas and hopes which have been the very life-blood of the faith. If we go with the other critical school, and hold fast to these life-giving hopes and ideas as the kernel of the matter, then we must lose the gracious human figure, so winning and so tender, which is, they tell us, but the myth in which the Idea has been enwrapped.

Are we caught in this horrible dilemma? Is there no way out of the snare? Ah! poor bewildered soul, distracted with sore amazement, there is one way, and one only, by which Christ need not be divided; by which the two halves come together, making of twain one perfect man; by which you retain *both* the forces which have, as a fact, built and established the faith—(1) the force of the spiritual ideal, (2) together with the force of the Gospel story. Both are yours, both are fused into one jet, both coalesce into a single simple fact, if only it be true, indeed, that the women did look into an empty tomb on that strange Easter morning long ago and saw no body there ; if it be true that two men did indeed rise out of their sorrow at the sudden news, and ran fast, and stooped down, and looked in, and saw the linen clothes lie, and the napkin that was round His head, not with the linen clothes, but laid rolled up by itself; if, indeed, by the side of a weeping woman who was possessed with but one thought, how to find the dead body of her Lord, it be true that there stood One Who said to her, "Mary ;" if, indeed, to two men journeying to Emmaus there was joined a third, Whose speech made their hearts burn, and Who was known in the breaking of bread ; if, indeed, through doors and walls, amid the trembling friends in that upper chamber in Jerusalem, there came again and yet again One Whose voice calmed them, Whose breath fell on them, Whose hands and side they saw ; if, indeed, by the lake, in the morning, there was a figure that drew near, and they knew it, and could not even ask themselves, in their wonder, "Is it the Lord?" knowing, as they did, that it was the Lord.

Oh, if this be but so, beloved, then, and then

alone, everything is clear, and consistent, and intelligible, and rational, and natural, and orderly. Natural and orderly! Yes, indeed, it is not the miracle of the Resurrection that causes unnatural disorder; it is its absence, its removal, that makes everything dislocated and irrational.

How whole and fitly framed together this earth of ours became to those who at the first saw and believed the Scriptures! How clear, intelligible, solid! Entanglement, contradiction—all were gone. They moved with freedom and gladness in a world of which they now held the key, over which they now found an easy mastery.

Oh that the scales might but fall from our eyes, and that we might see as they saw, and taste of their joy—the joy of seeing again their Lord, the joy which no man could again take from them! Oh that we might be no longer tossed about with every wind of doctrine; no longer hover round and round in vexed eddies of uncertainty; that we, who swore we would never believe it until we could put our hands into the print of the nails, might find ourselves confessing, "My Lord and my God"! How firm our tread would be, how rational our outlook, how deep our peace, if only it might be!

Yet we cannot believe it of ourselves; we cannot argue ourselves into it. Through the Spirit alone is faith made possible to us. Send down, then, send down on us, risen and ascended Master—send down Thy Holy Ghost, Thy Advocate, for Whom we wait! Touch our hearts, illuminate our reason, unseal our lips, that we also, by the faith of the operation of God, may become living witnesses to Thy Resurrection!

THE GOSPEL WITNESS.

"Whereof we all are witnesses."—ACTS ii. 32.

THAT is the key-note which the Apostles never tire of repeating. "You killed the Prince of Life, Whom God hath raised from the dead, whereof we all are witnesses." "God raised Him from the dead; and He was seen many days of them that came up with Him from Galilee to Jerusalem." "We are witnesses of all things which He did both in the land of the Jews, and in Jerusalem; Whom . . . God raised up the third day, and showed Him openly; not to all the people, but unto witnesses chosen before of God, even to us, who did eat and drink with Him after He rose from the dead."

"Witnesses of the Resurrection." "With great power gave the Apostles witness of the Resurrection of the Lord Jesus." And all this they did, in loyalty to His own prophetic Word: "Ye also shall bear witness, because ye have been with Me from the beginning."

"Whom God raised from the dead, whereof we all are witnesses." On this Apostolic witness the Church is built; and it may be well to recall how that Apostolic testimony has come down to us of to-day, and what grounds we have for asserting that we possess it in its adequate and authentic shape.

For, indeed, from the way people speak, I cannot but suppose that they are unaware of the results at which the criticism of the Gospels has finally arrived. They seem to think that the critical discussion of their authenticity has been increasingly disastrous; they are apparently perfectly ignorant of the strength of the case for the Gospels, which that discussion has increasingly disclosed. Forgive me, then, if I go over matters which may seem to many familiar and trite, and attempt to describe the situation which fifty years of intense and complete examination of our Apostolic witnesses have now secured to us.

What, then, is our authority for the Gospel narrative? To what centre, to what body of witnesses, to what date can we track it home? We used to suppose that the answer to such questions would turn entirely on the *written* Gospels—the books that are in our Bible. And, so supposing, we were annoyed to discover that it was exactly in the matter of the written record that our information was most hazy. When were they written down? Who exactly wrote them? Where were they written? How soon were they quoted? In all this we had but a few fragments of tradition to guide us—good enough tradition, but still slight, and indefinite, and lacking in precision; transmitted accidentally, as if not much trouble had been taken to certify it with warrantable names, facts, details. Above all, in date and place was the uncertainty at its height. And then we discovered also that direct quotations from these Gospels by name, and exact references to them, were strangely late, strangely long in coming; and it staggered us to hear that it is well on in the second century before we can positively assert that the Church is clearly using and quoting the very books as we have them in our hands to-day. It was at this point of the discussion that the critical results were most negative and most alarming, and it is at this antiquated point that much of the public popular mind still remains; so that even men of high reputation, in our first-class magazines, can talk of the Gospel story as " uncertified hearsay," and ask whether they are to accept the tremendous miracle of the Resurrection on evidence given a hundred years after it occurred, in books whose authorship and date are merely traditional.

Now, to use such language is to be grossly ignorant of the course later criticism has taken. For, as soon as we had recovered from the surprise of discovering this vagueness of certification for the written book, we looked closer; and we found at once, that this vagueness was due to the fact that the Christian Church did not dream of finding the first authority for its story in the written Word. It took it a hundred years to accustom itself to turn to these books as its primary authorities. Its earliest mind was strongly against writing. Writing was not its most natural method of preserving its story. It distrusted the accidents that beset it, the changes, the blunderings; it disliked the deadness of a dumb document. Our Lord had not written one word; He had definitely preferred to use living, human memories, written on the tablets of the heart; and the loyal impulses of the Church all set in the channels which He had marked down. Only very slowly, as the pressure of lengthening circumstances compelled her to face new possibilities, was she forced to see the necessity of depositing, in black and white, her witness to the Resurrection. And there can be no more convincing proof of her unwillingness to trust to writing than her own tradition that it was only when the death of the last Apostle grew ominously near that S. John could be induced to write down his record.

Here, then, was the real issue which criticism

had raised. It had shown how casually and how gradually the Church came into possession of her written story. But what did that prove? Did it prove that the story itself was casual, late, uncertified? that she was careless whence her story came to her? Far from it! It only proved that it was not in writings that we are to look for the authorized witness which the earliest Church warranted. She had other methods of giving and securing her testimony, which she preferred to writing. What, then, were those methods? Were they careful, reliable methods? Had they behind them certificated authority? Did the Church take heed how to secure to them this warrant?

What is the answer? Let us turn to the documents themselves and see. One of these Gospel writers has left on record the exact situation in which he wrote. He has told us what was his own title to write, and where his authority to do so lay. Nothing can be plainer or simpler, or better tally with what we have been saying. And we cannot doubt that his account of his own situation is common, certainly to S. Mark, himself a man of secondary rank, and probably to the written form of S. Matthew.[1]

S. Luke opens his Gospel with the familiar explanation. And see how important. First, his own name. Let us note that. We had imagined that all the validity turned on the authority of the particular writer: and when this was at all doubted or disputed, the story itself, we thought, lost all its warrant. But S. Luke never dreams of claiming such a position for himself. *He* is not the authority for the facts he narrates; he could not be. He, converted by S. Paul (so far as we know), could not be supposed to have seen anything himself; he had, probably, never seen the face of the Lord. He is in a wholly subordinate position. He is a careful, painstaking pupil, who has had exceptional opportunities of receiving the completer Christian instruction. That is why he proposes to write his Gospel; it will be a reliable record of what is

---

[1] The Gospel of S. John stands on a different footing altogether from the first three, and requires a separate treatment.

familiarly taught. But the story itself does not date itself from his book; far from it. It is perfectly well known already. Those for whom he writes it already know every word of it. Theophilus and he himself have sat together in the Christian schools, and have got it all by heart. The story exists long before it is written, and it is this existing story that has authoritative warrant. "Eye-witnesses of the facts" they were, who so taught it to S. Luke and his friend; "ministers of the Word," he calls them—certified personages whose peculiar and appointed office it was to bear the authentic witness. Here, in the background, lay the valid authority, on the strength of which the story was to be believed. On the word of these warranted men, Luke himself, and those for whom he wrote, already firmly believed it.

Why, then, is it written down? Simply for its permanent and trustworthy preservation in memory —to report it correctly. This humble task, which many were attempting, of copying out a correct and exact version of the things familiarly taught, of supplying a reliable and accurate report—this a devoted and attentive pupil like S. Luke had singular opportunities for fulfilling.

It is, then, behind him that his authority lies; and now the critical question divides itself into two: (1) What is known of this Gospel story which preceded the writings? Whither and to whom can we trace it? Is that story certified by adequate warrant? That is the all-important point. And, then, (2) Do our written Gospels correctly *report* this primitive and original story?

Now, each of these two questions, so divided, admits of an absolutely certain answer.

How can we trace the original Gospel story which the written Gospels are content to report? Let us go straight to our earliest sources of information.

Long before the story was written down, we have Christian documents which refer to it constantly; and these documents have this great merit, that, beyond all conceivable dispute or discussion, their exact authorship, date, occasion, meaning, are all determined. S. Paul's early epistles are the first form in which we possess the Apostolic witness. What notice do they give of a Gospel story? It is impossible to measure the vivid and habitual reference they make to it, until we have remembered a matter which we find it difficult to realize, *i.e.* that S. Paul, wherever he uses his favourite term of "my gospel," means by that word, not a theology, not a theory of Justification, but, primarily, the story of the Lord's Birth, Death, Resurrection, with its necessary interpretation. Take the salient instance 1 Cor. xv. 1. He speaks of a "gospel" which he "preached unto them," "wherein they stand," "by which they are saved," "if they hold it fast." What is it? What is this gospel which he received, which he delivered over to them? It is a record of facts; it is the assertion of certain historical events in their exact validity. It is the fact that "Christ died for our sins, ... rose again, ... was seen of Cephas, ... of the twelve, ... of James, ... of all the Apostles." That is the gospel, which, "whether it were I or they, so we preached, and so ye believed."

He refers again, in the eleventh chapter, to this solemn thing which he delivered, "which they received." What again is it? The fact that our Lord "on the night ... took bread." Cf. Rom. i. 1. What is the "gospel" to which S. Paul is "separated"? It is the same record of actual facts—the gospel of the Son, Who was born "of the seed of David according to the flesh; declared to be the Son of God with power, ... by the resurrection from the dead." And as it is grounded on sheer facts, so it terminates in a future fact—the fact that, on a certain day, God will judge the secrets of men's hearts by Jesus Christ, "according to my gospel." "Remember," he cries, with his last breath, "that Jesus Christ, of the seed of David, was raised from the dead, according to my gospel."[1]

This is his gospel—a story of the Lord's Life, presented in its absolute and world-wide significance; that He was born of a woman, under the Jewish law; that He died and was buried; that

---

[1] *Cf.* Gal. i. The "other gospel" is "another Jesus," *i.e.* a different presentation of the Historic Personality.

He rose again; that He will, on a certain day, judge the world. And this story is known, obviously, by heart to every soul to whom he writes. He can make the slightest possible references to it, with the absolute certainty of being understood. He recalls it to them in detail as the very groundwork of their lives, in the strength of which they stand and are saved; a thing known everywhere and by all, received and delivered in a manner they knew well, and from a source they knew well.

The Church possessed, then, in the years 54-56, a fixed and familiar story of the Lord. Whence did it get it? From whom was it received? Who were its authorities? Now, here we get on very sure ground. For the battle of S. Paul's career, as recorded in his earliest epistles, turns largely on this very point. What is that bitter *personal* controversy, which is ever coming to the surface, at Corinth, or in Galatia? Wherein lies its venom? Simply in this—that he brings a gospel, which, based as it is on definite historical events, can only be authorized by a certain definite body of men, who were alone privileged to give the testimony of selected and appointed eye-witnesses. These men were well known to all; they were that Apostolic company, established at Jerusalem, of whom the "chief pillars," the "notabilities," were Cephas, James, John. From them every gospel must come; every emissary who preaches it must carry their credentials. This is the prime necessity on which the security of the Church rests.

Who, then, is Paul, that he should authorize the Gospel? Does he bring such credentials? And, if not, how can he deliver it? If he may preach it, then it can only be as an agent, acting under the authority of the Twelve. But, then, what claim has he to found Churches, to stand to them as Apostles alone can stand?

Here is the point on which the opposition takes its stand. And we can still feel clearly enough, in the strain and fervour of S. Paul's language, how strong the case against him looked, how convincing and clear were the positions taken. And we can measure by that how firm and rooted were the assumptions on which the arguments against him rested. The heat and passion of that terrible struggle have burned itself into the epistles that record it; but that agony of S. Paul will not have been in vain, or without compensating fruit to the Church, if it abides as an overwhelming evidence to us to-day, of the rigorous care which the earliest Church took in securing valid testimony to its Gospel story.

From one source alone can it allow that story to come; the standing of its teachers turns wholly on their right relation to that source.

And, now, what is that source? It is the Twelve, permanently fixed at Jerusalem, headed by Cephas, James, John. The witness is given by a selected, official, certified body—"the witnesses chosen before of God," "ordained to be witnesses of the Resurrection"—carefully defined, set apart for this particular function from out of those who were with the Lord from one fixed date, the Baptism of

John, to another, the Ascension.[1] And it is given at Jerusalem ; *i.e.* the men who claim to have seen the event with their own eyes make that claim in the very spot and scene where, as they say, it took place. From this spot they refuse to move. They are witnesses to a fact, and the only fit place where that witness can be given is there where it could best be confuted. There they stand—the heart of the witnessing Church ; and round them the whole organization of the Church frames itself—frames itself as an organization to carry their certified story abroad, along authentic and authorized channels ; so that far away in Asia Minor, and in Achaia, and in Rome, there shall be but one test for all teachers—" What are your relations to the notables, the pillars, the Apostolic teachers at Jerusalem ? "

The one taunt against S. Paul is, " You are trying to rebel against that supreme authority."

And observe, that the taunt has such a sting in it, just because S. Paul's " Gospel story " is identical with that taught by the Twelve. That is why his

[1] Acts i. 21, 22.

foes can challenge him with being a mere emissary from the Apostles at Jerusalem. And he is careful to allow that he and the Twelve have been in communication. It is true (he must admit it) that he went up to Jerusalem to make earnest inquiries of S. Peter; only he pleads that that was not necessary to his authority, which is proved by his not going up for three years. Again, at another time, fourteen years later, he consented, "lest he should run in vain," and his work be broken up, to lay his own Gospel story by the side of theirs; and they found nothing amiss in it—nothing to add or diminish. As to the Gospel itself, as told by him and by them, there was absolute identity; only they agreed to separate ministries. S. Paul's story, then, is the story told by Peter, James, and John at Jerusalem.

And now we can measure, from other sources, the strict importance which these Apostles attributed to their essential office of authorizing the story. For we are told in the Acts that, as soon as the work of the Church grew, they singled out two functions to which they limited themselves, resigning into other hands all business which interfered with these two; and these were—(1) worship; (2) the ministry of the Word, and that is, in fact, simply the teaching of the Lord's life, the imbedding in the living memory, through the machinery of catechetical schools, the events which S. Peter sums up in his vivid speeches—" Jesus of Nazareth, a man approved of God by mighty works and wonders; Him the Jews crucified and slew; Him God raised up; and of this we are witnesses."

Those schools are coeval with the Church; and so vital was it for the Apostles to stand at Jerusalem and deliver this witness to the Church, that absolutely their first act, on finding themselves alone, is to complete their full number, that the testifying body may be entire and four-square; and we know, by S. Peter's speech, how painstaking they were to secure that the new man shall be wholly qualified as a reliable eye-witness. So vital, again, was it to abide in the one spot of testimony, that we are startled to find them abandoning active missionary work, for the sake of retaining the solid witnessing force at the centre. That is why so little seems to have been done by the Twelve themselves in spreading the Gospel abroad.

And consider the length of time covered by the dates of which we are speaking. S. Paul, in the Epistle to the Galatians, carries us back to the year 37, for his own conversion, at the very latest; and before his conversion comes his persecution, witnessing to the story then told by these same men. There, in Jerusalem, the Twelve stood then; seventeen years later, they are still there; at the date of the Epistle to the Corinthians, there they are yet to be found—Cephas, James, John. For twenty-five years, at least, after the facts which they assert, they remain making that assertion in Jerusalem itself; they only drag themselves away when the gathering siege forces them to flight. Then, at last, as that scattering of the witnessing band becomes imminent, is the story seemingly entrusted to written records, which may compensate for the possible loss of the living instruction. But by this time the story has been long and firmly rooted; the written Book is intended only to secure it to the believing memory; while everywhere and for ever two pillars have been set up, which will perpetuate the living authority of that Apostolic witness: (1) the pillar of the Creed, ever rehearsed before God in public assembly, ever committed to the instructed heart of every single convert—in itself nothing but a shortened gospel, a positive summary of certain historic facts, which took place at a fixed date, at a certified historical moment—"under Pontius Pilate;" and (2) the pillar of the Worship, of which the central act enshrines the perpetuated memory of a certain night, the very night in which the Master was betrayed; when He did that which the Gospel story records, which all had received, which all had had delivered down to them—"that our Lord Jesus Christ took bread, and gave thanks," and bade them rehearse that act for ever "in memory of Him."

Here, then, is our testimony. We are asked where, when, and from what witnesses our story was first delivered. Our answer is both secure and complete. The Gospel story of our Lord's Life, Death, and Resurrection was most certainly told to the Church by a knot of living men, selected as eye-witnesses for this very purpose; selected according to definite rules, with a defined purpose, that they might tell this story. They told it, headed by three great names, Peter, John, and James, the Lord's own brother, at Jerusalem, the spot where the facts occurred; they told it in full consciousness of the importance of securing warranted accuracy. We note how careful, how definite, how formal are the pains spent on the certification of the living witness, as contrasted with the vague uncertainties which surround the origin of the written records. We are in presence of men who recognize, with all their might, the urgency of the task set them. They are bent on securing this valid, and formal, and official witness, from the very first hour of their being left alone; their earliest act was to fill up their total strength of testimony; they gave themselves up to the task of securing the living memory of this story throughout the whole Church. They were accepted by all as its sole authorities, S. Paul being only added to their number, in the face of furious opposition, on the distinct ground that his witness was first-hand even as theirs, and his story identical with theirs. They had a special class of officers set apart to carry their story abroad in its certified and authentic form, called Evangelists. And all this they did, not for some broken moments, but continuously from the very first year following our Lord's death, for at least twenty-five years on end, in that one place where all could best be confuted. On the reality of this story they rested their whole case; on this witness of the Twelve the Church's foundations were laid. Round about this Apostolic witness, the whole organization of the Christian body was framed; the continuity of the Apostolic organization is for the sake of preserving the unbroken continuity of the testimony. On that story, on a statement of historical facts, the Creed is built and the worship fashioned; round that story the entire Church is grouped.

Men talk lightly and ignorantly of "uncertified hearsay." Would it be possible to use a phrase which would describe the facts more wrongly, or contradict them more perversely? The entire Church exists for the sake of certifying to the testimony, for the sake of testifying to the truth and validity of the facts; the Church exists in order to bear its warranted witness that Jesus Christ was indeed "born of the Virgin Mary, suffered under Pontius Pilate," "was raised the third day from the dead," "whereof we all are witnesses."

There remains our second question. Granting that this Gospel story, so originated and vouched, was known by heart to the entire Church from the year 34 onward, do our written Gospels correctly report to us what that story was? That is a very simple question, and it permits of a very plain, simple, and certain answer. For not only has the course of criticism absolutely justified their supreme excellence, regarded as a *report* of the current and earliest story; but we are saved from all troublesome discusssion of the probabilities of their accuracy, by this simple fact, that, as to whether or no those writings correctly *reported* the certified story, the Church itself was in a position to judge. It knew the story as it was told and taught by the warranted witnesses; and in that knowledge it approved and adopted those Gospels—approved and adopted them with such unhesitating and world-wide decision, that all other attempts at writing it down were surrendered, and vanished. A Church that had taken such persistent pains to secure, from the first, that it had hold of the story from the authentic sources, cannot conceivably have adopted inadequate reports of what it familiarly knew.

"Whereof we all are witnesses." It was the earliest and the highest office of the Church to bear testimony, to give proofs, to warrant its Creed. That is still its primary office, its most urgent task. It is itself to be the strong assurance before men that the Gospel story is a true record of fact. To anoint it to this office, the Spirit of God came down at Pentecost, and abides in the heart of the Church for ever. And it is for testimony, for proofs, that men are now asking—asking with scorn, with cruelty, with carelessness sometimes, but asking, far more often, in an agony of dread, under the sway of an intellectual panic, which is felt creeping over them like a contagion, as a plague-breath that chills, and unnerves, and paralyzes, and sickens. Testimony, evidence, proof, witness—for these they anxiously, feverishly ask. To give these is no accident of our Christian life; it is the very essence and aim of our membership in Christ's Body.

And we can offer our witness with a glad confidence; for we can most assuredly track back, with absolute certainty, to a warranted, and certified, and authentic source, that story which is the very core of our personal lives to-day.

But yet, let us ever repeat and remind them and ourselves, it must still be " the Spirit that beareth witness "—the Spirit that, through us, testifies, and convinces, and wins. What does that involve? The evidence we offer can never be mathematical, formal, dead. It can never be worked out as an algebraical formula, as a proposition of Euclid, as a piece of experimental science; for the facts of which we offer proof are historical—that is, they are human, they are living. The probability of their occurring will turn entirely on our personal estimate of human life and of its possibilities, its heights and its depths, its character and its aims, its origin and its end. And what that estimate will be must always depend on our spiritual condition.

Such evidence as we offer speaks from Spirit to spirit, from God to man. And if, therefore, we have already, under an intellectual panic, surrendered our consciousness of a spiritual world above, around, beneath us, which can touch, and help, and lift us, then no external evidence can ever restore our nerves, or lay hold of our imagination, or win our confidence, or move our rational assent.

Have we such a spirit-world, above, around, beneath us, wide, open, illimitable, in the heart of which this mighty deed of God in Christ takes place, "by which He raised Jesus from the dead"? A spirit-world, far, far above our heads, wherein lies heaven and its thousand times ten thousand? A spirit-world, deep down below our feet, wherein is the darkness of the pit, and sin, and death, and that old serpent the devil, and the abyss of wrath? A spirit-world, around us, in face of us, wherein is God our Father—God, not idle or remote, but near, active, invoking, pursuing, persuading, beseeching, opening to us His Heart of Love, made new, made our own in the pity and tenderness of Jesus? A spirit-world, unveiled by the ministering motions of the Holy Spirit? Have we such a world as this: and are we looking out into it, not with the cold, hard inspection of a critical and unconcerned spectator, but with the eyes of a human spirit, personal, alive, profoundly interested; with a spirit that seeks a heavenly country, a spirit that is weighted with the sense of its own infirmity, a spirit that knows the awful shadow of spiritual wrong?

So we must be looking, according to this measure of our destiny, according to this standard of its possibilities, if ever we are to judge the witness of the Spirit that God has raised Jesus from the dead. So looking, so judging, and so alone, can the way be thrown open by which the Spirit of God may descend and find a way to our souls, and may take of the things of Christ and show them unto us. So alone can we have at last the witness in our own hearts—that sweet unction from the Holy Spirit of Pentecost by which we may "know all things."

THE ELEMENTAL ENIGMAS.

"We have seen and do testify that the Father sent the Son to be the Saviour of the world."—1 JOHN iv. 14.

ALL those, and they are very many, who have read the Life of Charles Darwin have felt the instinctive fascination of that high character. Never, surely, has a life been told which left a more engaging picture on the memory. His bright geniality, his delightful companionableness, his simple nobility, his domestic kindliness—these are notes that speak home to English hearts. There is nothing that charms an Englishman so surely as the sight of supreme gifts and magnificent fame, which yet are totally devoid of all posing, all artificiality, all vanity, and are worn lightly and easily, with the honest and homely simplicity of a man who finds himself able to do something very great for his fellows, and does it as modestly and quietly as if it were the commonest and humblest duty in the world. Shakespeare has left us an ideal here of the bearing and behaviour of genius, which we are not likely to forget; and we take it to our hearts whenever, as in Charles Darwin, we recognize this touch of the national spirit.

And how complete in him the happy portrait is! So patient, and steady, and careful he is in the slow preparation of his great idea; so absolutely true in his deliberate consideration of all that makes against it; so trustful in his quiet certainty that the difficulties which baffle him will be found to disappear; so exquisitely tempered, both in his gay chivalry to his theory, and yet in his graceful deference to his two dear yet unconvinced friends. Never, surely, was a new position fought for with more consummate self-control and such unbroken geniality. And then the limitless success, the overwhelming honour of the victory, never, for one moment, ruffle the sweet, simple, good-humoured honesty of the man. Pleasant, human, modest, he remains to the last wholly what he had ever been.

No vice seems to come over him; life's conditions are amiable and honourable from start to close; no flaw thwarts the graceful, friendly, hearty presence. It is a delightful record.

And why is it, then, that, as we lay it down, we are vexed with a vague sense of bewilderment? We have to reflect, to draw upon ourselves, in order to discover; and, so reflecting, we see why we are puzzled. For we have been absorbed in the interest and the nobility of a man's life, from out of which have utterly vanished the two elemental enigmas which lie at the base of all our spiritual history. The philosophical enigma, the moral enigma —these do not appear in the drama of Darwin's days. Of course no one can effect a gigantic revolution in scientific thought without coming across the intellectual questions which beset our knowledge of reality. Darwin finds himself challenged, compelled to say something—to declare what he holds about ultimate truth. But this challenge is forced on him from outside. There is no sign at all of his being himself the least bit in touch with speculative problems. His own scientific formula has this especial merit, that it succeeds in separating off the proper and peculiar ends which science has in view, from all those ulterior questions to which philosophy and religion apply themselves; it enables these ultimate questions to be put by, to be held in reserve, to be dismissed from the immediate business in hand. And this dismissal once clearly accomplished, all difficulty for Darwin is over.[1] He is never the least afflicted or perplexed by the problems that concern the reality of the objects that we know, or of the subject that knows them. He confesses himself totally uninterested in such metaphysical questions. No shadow of intellectual uneasiness discolours his radiant world of fact. His good, bright, eager mind is wholly captivated with the intense enjoyment of scientific observation, experiment, discovery. And there he ends. Young men, full of anxious problems, thrust

[1] He confesses himself exercised over the question of "design" in Nature: but this question concerns the practical, rather than the speculative, intellect.

upon him their own turmoil, and he has, when pressed, to call himself an "Agnostic." But the big name covers no deep philosophical position; it only means the mental temper and attitude of an honest and cheerful Englishman, to whom and for whom these burning questions do not practically or vitally exist.

And as with the intellectual, so with the moral enigma. For that smooth, even, upright career, it too does not exist. No hot breath of struggle; no cruelty of passion; no stubbornness of the rebel will; no selfish egotism; no encrusted pride; no torturing vanity; no inward misery at some deep, silent sore; no fretting wilfulness; no profound hunger after a peace that has been lost. No! there is no sense of wrong; no curse; hardly even an effort—so easy, so straight, so happy is his path. Looking back from out of the very shadow of death at his fair and sunny days, he can call up no remorse, he tells us, for any great sin; only he can just wish he had done a little more good in the world.

Nor does his experience of men throw any blight on this broad cheerfulness. He had a chivalrous ardour against the harshness of slavery, the one instance of social evil with which he came in contact. But his habits kept him far aloof from all that is gross, fierce, base, horrible. Encompassed by loving friends, himself one of the most lovable of men, he passes from youth to manhood, from manhood into the dignity of old age, without check or hitch, without slur or damage; and when he is laid in his honourable grave, has the accuser of his brethren anything at all that he can lay against him?

The enigmas of human life, the intellectual and the moral enigmas—these have disappeared; and no wonder that we are bewildered at such immense omissions in a character of such supreme value.

And yet, even though such a case bewilder us, it will at least relieve us of an earlier trouble which probably daunted us. We had, perhaps, supposed that we had to count the whole force of Mr. Darwin's mind as against us in our Christian belief. We had darkly wondered to ourselves why it was that the greatest scientific intellect of the day should see no justification for our creed. We knew our own smallness, our narrow intellectual gift; we admired his splendid powers; how is it that our faith and the evidences of our faith, if they, indeed, be true and strong, do not commend themselves to a man of this high capacity and excellent judgment? Can that be a revelation from God which, however forcibly it appeals to us, cannot win its way to the greatest and purest intellect of the day? Such questions lurk about us very deeply; they cow and daunt our faith, even when it seems to us firm; for they throw a cloud of suspicion over our own powers of judgment. How can we trust our own faculties, however sure their report, if the experience of another, who is of infinitely superior weight, contradicts ours? So our belief creeps into its shell, and cowers, and fears to assert itself, and loses its nerve.

What a relief, then, to discover that this other had never had the experiences to which we make our primary appeal; was not ever in possession of the facts which are to us so convincing; that he had not travelled into the country of which we are talking! What a relief to find that he has never given judgment against our creed, simply because the matters that constitute its justification never fell within his range and horizon! It is as if we, who were being ravished with some melodious music, had been disturbed at noticing another listener, who remained totally unconcerned and inattentive, without a sign of emotion on his face; so that we were dumbfounded, and had begun to question our own delight and to distrust our own taste, and to wonder whether that by which we were fascinated could indeed be so beautiful, if it left another's heart so absolutely untouched; and were then suddenly to discover that he was stone-deaf. Back with a rush would come our confidence, our security; his unconcern would cease even to throw a shadow of suspicion on our joy. So in the case of Charles Darwin. We may, indeed, wonder at the limitations of human genius, which seem to be set it by the very conditions of its development, so that supreme excellence and energy in one department may be purchased at the cost of absolute quiescence in other directions. But, at any rate, we know where we stand as to the evidence and credentials of our faith; we understand why they should have so little effect there, where the case to which they apply does not exist. For an answer is sure to look futile to the man who has never asked the question to which it responds. A solution cannot commend itself when the problem which it solves has never been felt. A hazardous and tremendous effort at a rescue is bound to seem silly and uncalled for by those who recognize no peril to which they are liable.

And, as we know well, the entire justification of Christianity lies in those twin enigmas, which were so strangely absent from this great life of which we have been speaking. Christianity assumes that those enigmas are at the very root of a man's spiritual existence. It assumes that round them his whole spiritual history turns. It assumes that man's primary and vital office is to know God, to know the ultimate Truth of truths, to know the Very God. It assumes that man is aware that he ought to be capable of this high achievement, and that his inner motions are all bent on achieving it, and that he will at all hazards seek, and ask, and knock; that he will have ever in his soul the quickening cry, "O that I knew where I might find Him, that I might come into His presence;" that he will press hither and thither, urged by an unceasing hunger, as he makes his one importunate demand on all who can teach, "Show us the Father, and it sufficeth us." Christianity assumes all this, and assumes that man, nevertheless, cannot, by this searching, find out God; cannot come into His presence; cannot see with his eyes and hear with his ears that which he is for ever pursuing;—cannot, because he has lost the thread, has confused the track, has got entangled and perplexed; so that the distinctions between creature and Creator have vanished, and all has become hazy, and miserable, and harassing, and ineffectual. And, moreover, it assumes that this intellectual impotence is knit up, as man finds, with some horrible moral wrong, which perverts his insight, and blurs his vision, and defeats his judgment, and yet cannot be undone, or abandoned, or cured; nay, which gathers increase out of his intellectual confusion, and deepens and darkens as his knowledge of God grows more chaotic, and roots itself ever firmer as his hold on spiritual truth loosens. And so the wrong ever worsens, and the weakness ever spreads, and the disease ever sickens; and man, who was made to know God, and, in knowing Him, to become holy as God is holy, lapses day by day further and further from the capacity to know Him, and day by day, therefore, sinks lower under the weight of sin, and falls further and yet further from the holiness of God, and becomes ever less able to commune with God, or to bring his life into the searching light of the Holy Presence.

All this is assumed before Christianity can begin. And it is assumed, not arbitrarily, not fancifully, not speculatively, so that it can be confounded by some stray and rare instances, where all this assumption finds no counterpart; but on the invincible evidence offered by the history of two thousand years—the history of man's best and purest efforts to attain this knowledge; the history especially of one immense, and prolonged, and stubborn attempt that was inaugurated by Abraham, the father of the faithful, and was carried on by Moses, and Samuel, and David, and Isaiah, and Ezekiel, and Ezra, and was embodied in the entire story of a nation, and was recorded in psalm, and chronicle. and prophet, and on which were spent the blood of heroes, and the devotion of priests, and the patience of martyrs, and the love of saints. There is the overwhelming evidence which nothing can shake. The case has been proved out and out, long ago. S. Paul had complete right to sum up the whole situation: "by ... the Law"—by things as they stand—can "no flesh be justified." Man ought to know God, yet he cannot; man ought to be holy, yet it is impossible. O miserable man, what shall deliver him?

That is the question of questions, to which the Resurrection of Jesus Christ is the one answer. Only, to understand, to estimate the answer, you must first have asked the question. That is what we mean by calling Christianity historical, by speaking of its preparation. It is historical; it appears at one hour, not at another—at an hour in which man's history has arrived at a certain critical entanglement. It comes to meet certain conditions, a certain situation, in which a long past has resulted. Except in relation to that situation, it is, of course, unintelligible; except as releasing man from that critical entanglement, it is, of course, unjustifiable. It has a preparation; and any who would understand it must have travelled along the road that leads up to it, must have undergone that preparatory discipline.

Christianity arrived in the world in face of the pressure of these enigmas. Is this pressure, my brethren, less to-day than it was then? The intellectual enigma, for instance: Man is made to know God, and yet fails to know Him. That was the verdict, the summing-up of S. Paul, on the state of human wisdom before the Resurrection: "The world by its wisdom knew not God." Would he be at all inclined to change or modify that verdict to-day? Would he see any reason to reconsider it? Alas! has not the evidence in its favour multiplied a thousandfold in the years that have passed since he spoke? So that now, to-day, at the end of all our seeking to find God, we find, on every side, that men are so despairing of success in the search that they are seriously doubting whether the search ought ever to have been made—whether it be not true that man was never made to know God. All around us reason is in retreat. It is surrendering problem after problem; it is abandoning position after position; it is shutting itself up within the narrow boundaries of its own unexplained experience, and refusing to venture out a step beyond that walled fortress. It fears to trust itself; it makes no claims to know anything. It names itself Agnostic; and that means that it throws up the cards, that the game is lost. All its ancient heroic ventures into the unseen, the real, the true, the absolute—these are over. It capitulates ; it resigns itself to accept its own ignorance ; it deems it useless to prolong the struggle. Nothing can be known as it is. Why do we talk of the *progress* of intellect? Surely the intellect of the day is in full retreat from out of all the country it once claimed to occupy. It is openly professing defeat. It can find no road, as it once hoped, out of its own limited horizon, out beyond the range of its local and earthly faculties. Man was not made to know the reality of things ; man cannot know God. This is the melancholy message which reason is enforcing.

Yet, to accept it is to commit suicide ; to accept it is to stifle all spiritual aspiration, to slit the nerves of all human hope. To accept it is to close our Bible for ever, to confess that the entire movement recorded in the Bible—from the first call of Abraham down to the last farewell of S. John— was a childish and aimless blunder; that patriarch, and prophet, and apostle have simply led the world astray on a false scent; that our Lord has carried the madness of man to its height when He told us that in Him we do know God. For us, such a confession is impossible; such an act of suicide is forbidden; for we stand by the belief that to know God is eternal life. We anyhow cannot escape the enigma by denying that there is one. We cannot bring our Bibles to be burned.

And yet, if man is ever to know God, there is at this moment but one road left open, there is but one offer for him to consider. For all other claimants are retiring; they are eagerly professing their inability to open him a way into the ultimate truth. Only one claimant remains, challenging us to follow Him. It is He Who has risen; Who has passed out beyond our earthly boundaries, beyond our temporal experiences, beyond our limited horizon, and has broken through the gates of brass and smitten the bars of iron asunder that so cruelly curb our vision. It is He Who has gone up into the land beyond death, the reality beyond the show; gone up into the very abyss of God; yet, so going, seated at the very heart of God's eternal power, He still is what we know Him to be, still wears the nature which we understand, still is intelligible to our head and our heart; and still He cries to us out of the centre of the abyss, "If ye know Me, ye know My Father also; he who sees Me sees the Father; for I am in the Father, and the Father in Me."

In knowing Christ, ascended to God's right hand, we know God Himself. That is the glorious fruit of the Resurrection which we celebrate to-day.[1] For to-day is the feast of that knowledge of God that has been won by the Resurrection. Carried into God through the Christ, following up into the Godhead the flesh-bearing Jesus Whom we know and love, we have a medium through which the light of God Himself can pass to us—can pass undiminished, unblurred, undistorted, through the mediation of Him Who, known to us in the flesh, is yet "Very God of Very God." He Who sees the Very God pledges Himself to us that the know-

[1] Preached on Trinity Sunday.

ledge He gives us of God is real—that in seeing Him we do indeed see the Father. And so, out of the Resurrection, there slowly has broken out upon us, from the abyss of heaven, that mighty truth about God which gives its name to this Sunday—the teaching of the Trinity, which is the translation into thought of the truth that "God is love," which was declared to us in His raising Jesus Christ from the dead. "God is love:" a Being Whose essence is built up in loving relationships— in a Father Who, out of eternal love, begets a Son; in a Son Who, in eternal love, gives back to the Father His own blessed image; in a Spirit Who proceeds, in love, from each, and in love takes of each and gives to the other. Here is indeed a solution of the intellectual enigma, "We must know God, yet we cannot;" for it meets the dilemma full and fair in the words, "No man hath seen God at any time; nevertheless, the only begotten Son, Who is in the bosom of the Father, He hath revealed Him to us;" He Who is lifted up into the glory which He had before the world, has taken the Name of the Father and manifested it unto us.

And the moral enigma—the dark curse of moral impotence, the misery of seeing the better and doing the worse—that black enigma still encompasses us with no less terror, yea, rather with a deeper depression than in the days when S. Paul read out its secret. And from that dismal depression who is able to release himself, unless Christ be now alive at the right hand of God, seated in power, and hath "all things in subjection under His feet"? "If Christ be not raised ye are yet in your sins." The awful dilemma—"still in our sins." If Christ has not risen, then the weight of woe has never been lifted off the earth, the mastery of the evil tradition has never been broken, the entail never been cut off. The ancient wrong, so strong and rooted, has never suffered defeat. The tyranny is unshaken; nay, it is established yet firmer, since it overcame Christ, the Champion of God, and beat down into a bloody grave the fairest, purest, noblest soul that ever breathed.   If Christ has never been raised, then the world has never been overcome as He promised; the prince of this world has never been judged; the strong man who holds us in miserable possession has never been bound; the blow has never been struck which broke the iron bars; the honour and Name of God have never been vindicated.

And if so, then that tremendous picture drawn by S. Paul, of the world before Christ, is still the only conclusion.   Evil is slowly and steadily winning. There is no man who can give it the lie, can wrestle with it and survive.   No, not one.   The set of sin is too mighty; the flood is ever rising, and there is no saving act of God that has come in to withstand it.

And we!   We, then, have no buoyant hope of victory behind us; no blessed assurance, in the midst of our tribulation, that He Who is our Captain hath already, long ago, overcome the world.   No!   Struggle as we may against the hateful thing, the battle has gone against us.   We are on the beaten side; we are under the doom of a moral defeat; we shall not have the force, or the courage, or the nerve, or the purity to carry the fight through. We shall fall. For there are weak spots in our armour; there are bad memories within, treacherous and cowardly; there are wounds and sores which will break out under this fierce strain. Those only have any confidence who have never tasted our cup, never known our anguish, never been touched with our infirmities. Some few such there are, rare souls, who are sunny and of good cheer, because some happy chance has lifted them sheer out of the battle and has spared them all the strain. One such we have been now remembering. But such a confidence can never be ours. For we know what the battle means—its tremendous heat, its endless onset; and we know our own faint-heartedness, our own inadequacy, our own taint, our own treachery. "We are yet in our sins if Christ be not raised." "Yet in our sins." We may fight on; but in our camp there is no cry of victory, no shout of a king, and we fight as those that sadly foreknow the inevitable end.

H

We may hope, struggle, but it will be in vain; the thrust of evil will be too strong for us. We shall yield; we shall break at last; we shall sink; we shall go under; and, when we die, we shall leave behind us an earth that still groans as heavily as of old, under the same tyrannous empire of wrong—an earth that ever darkens down under a sorrow that can never be appeased.

Here, then, is the moral issue that depends on Christ's Resurrection. You and I, in our conflict with an old sin, deep-seated and strong—a sin that is wound into our very being, that has dug its fangs into our flesh, that has poisoned our spiritual springs—under what conditions are we fighting? That is a very vital, a very critical question. Are we fighting with the assurance of victory—the assurance that God has Himself struck the great triumphant blow on our side, in that He raised Jesus Christ from the dead? Are we fighting in the sure consciousness that the yoke of the oppressor is broken; that it cannot hold us fast bound in our misery and crime; that the fetters must fall ; that the horrid snake of sin must loosen its coils if we but endure bravely ; that all power in heaven and earth is ours, since we are Christ's, and Christ is God ; that already we have in us the hope and pledge of invincible purity, so that nothing can ever compel us to fall so long as we are but faithful ; that within us the Spirit of God wars gallantly; that above us the prevailing intercession of the Son ever proceeds ; that ever and again, as the sin renews its power and makes new inroads and stains us with fresh defilement, the Blood of Jesus is sprinkled over us to cleanse us from all our sins ; that ever the Blessed Father bends over us with shielding love, as He sees in us the image and the face of His Son ? Is that our battle ? Are those our succours ? They are so only if Christ rose the third day from the dead.

Do we say, "Ah! how slow and poor the winnings, even if all this be true " ? Well, let us measure, by that poverty of our slow and scanty victory, what our defeat would be if those succours were all withdrawn, if all that hope had fled out of our days, if that blow for God had never been struck, if Christ had never been raised! Alas! if with all this belief we get forward so little, how utter, how dark the collapse if all that makes victory not incredible, not hopeless, were gone!

Look deep into our own sick hearts. Look out, far and wide, over the groaning earth. Can we doubt on which side the victory will lie "if Christ be not raised"? For, indeed, there are ominous signs about us—menaces of a vast moral overthrow. The day may be upon us when evil shall come in as a flood. Where shall we be, if the Lord have indeed raised no standard against it? Believe me, this is no mere question whether a miraculous fact did, or did not, take place long ago. It is a matter of life or death to our spiritual hopes to-day, whether or not, as we faintly push forward against the terrible forces of sin, we have behind us the powers of the Triune God, pledged to our eternal succour by the Resurrection of Jesus Christ; whether or no He, our Risen Lord, now holds the keys of death; whether or no the issues of the fray are all in His hands; whether or no we can count on it, in the blind heat of the battle, that He sees and knows how we fare, and what we need, and invokes the Father's love upon us, and feeds us with the Spirit's consolation.

Without this, who dares hope? With this, who dares fail?

CORPORATE FAITH.

"Holding the Head, from which all the body by joints and bands having nourishment ministered, and knit together, increaseth with the increase of God."—COL. ii. 19.

WE all are apt to roughly contrast with one another the inner acts of individual faith, and the outer system, or Church, into which those individual believers are grouped. So contrasted, we can argue for ever as to the relative importance, authority, validity, predominance of the one element or the other. Who can ever decide on their true proportions to one another? From one point of view, the individual believers seem but as the stones of a vast and beautiful building, which embodies the mind and enshrines the honour of God. They are but as leaves, which come, and flourish, and die, while the tree endures, and grows, and spreads its branches far and wide. They are but the tools and material which the kingdom of God, come on earth, puts to its own high uses. The interest, the heart, the thought, all are bent on passing beyond the mere detail of personal conversion, fascinating as its study may be in its proper proportion and place; and on realizing, and interpreting, and formulating, and embracing the great issues of the world's redemption—the unchanging and unresting work which the Father and the Son and the Spirit push forward through all time.

And against all this the other side is strenuously pleading: "This Church, after all, is but an instrument for the saving of individual souls. Out of these alone can it be formed; for the sake of these alone it lives and works; these are its prizes, its jewels, its resources, its fruit. In the inward soul of man lies all spiritual worth. No system, however splendid, can be so precious as this, for from this it draws its own value. The inward soul, in its struggle, its faith, its conversion, its sanctity—with this alone, in the final resort, is God concerned. In this alone does the

Son see of the travail of the Spirit, and is satisfied. All else is machinery—some devised by man, some allowed by God for purposes of human expediency; much of it useful, good—yes, even necessary. But, for all that, it is quite secondary, temporary, subservient. It no doubt serves to extend the opportunities for faith, to secure the results of faith, to satisfy the natural sympathies of the faithful. Men who believe naturally desire to come together, to combine, to co-operate. But the reality, the essence, of religion is not to be found in this. It must all yield before the dominant, the incomparable interest of the personal soul, in its solitary and secret hold upon the life that is given it in Jesus Christ."

Now, there is the outline of an argument that, so stated, can never reach a solution; for it must always depend on our own private character and aptitudes to which side we will give the preference, to which interest we shall ascribe the predominance. But what if the whole question were, in that form, a mistake? What if the entire discussion ought to be taken a stage further back, and, instead of contrasting the inward and the outward, the personal faith and the Church system, pitting them one against the other, as if they were two rival elements, different in kind, antithetical, contradictory, which were brought into artificial combination with one another, we were to ask, " What is this personal faith? What is its character, its constitution, its nature?" It is true (we allow it frankly) that everything lies in personal faith. The living soul of the believer—this is no doubt the one thing needful, the one thing of worth; here is the root, the base, the focus, the scene, the aim of all these marvellous workings of the Spirit. The system is nothing, is worthless, except so far as it has living, believing souls, in whom, and through whom, and for whom it exists. Yes, inner personal faith; that is the root-secret. But let us examine this faith as it is in the individual believer. Is it private because it is personal? Is it solitary because it is individual? What is faith? If we recall its character, as it is portrayed in the language of the Gospels, or analyzed by the spiritual insight of S. Paul, is it an act which can be conceived of as isolated, separate, alone? Can you describe or name it in any words which can succeed in confining its action to the secrecy of the separate and solitary soul? For is it not in its very essence, according to the language of Christ and His Apostles, an act of admittance into a body—the Body of Christ? Is it not an act through which the soul is newly begotten—begotten into a race; born of God into a holy fellowship, into the very heart of a kingdom, into the very thick of a holy people, into a blessed company of the elect, into membership, into companionship, into citizenship, into a corporate and compact society, into the new, the spiritual Jerusalem? The soul that believes, that lays hold of Christ, is by that very act introduced into the relationships of the new body.

But if this be the full conception of faith, then personal faith and the society, the Church, do not stand contrasted, in antithesis to one another.

But rather the act of faith, which takes place within the inner recesses of the individual soul, has already within it the character of the citizen of heaven, the germ, the construction, the instinct, the fashion, the features, the sympathies, the powers, the capacities of the body into which it has been called. It is already intended for a place in that body; it is created with a view to that companionship; it is already alive with possible attachments, relationships, intimacies, correlations, by which it is prepared for insertion within that close and compacted whole. That which makes it faith must make it also capable of intercourse, of society, of brotherhood. It cannot be the one without being the other. The act which begets it endows it also with the conditions by which it can pass into the assembly of the firstborn, into the great company of the saints. To be saved is to be made one of many. By the act of belonging to God, the soul belongs to its fellows; for it is incorporated with Christ, Who is one and the same in all. The soul that believes must, therefore, have all this social and public character hidden within it; so that, if we could conceive it, for instance, placed alone under a spiritual microscope and examined by some scientific eye that was able to read its secret, it would be said, "This is a creature that belongs, evidently, to some larger whole. Its construction proves that it is adapted for social intercourse; it has in it the ligatures, and joints, and sinews by which it could be knit up into an articulated body. It would be possible to suggest the probable construction of that larger body by close examination of this fragment." Faith—personal, private faith, as it exists in the individual soul—is surely something of this kind. Every word used to describe it implies the coexistence, the correlation, the adherence of the several believers. How can we read the Epistle to the Colossians without acknowledging that, to the Apostolic mind and imagination, faith always implies and involves a body, an order of relationships, a regulated system of combination, a holy society, a spiritual Church?

And if this is its inherent nature, then it must

surely be provided with some actual means of realizing on earth this its original and mystical character. Unless it can obtain this, it is maimed; it is curtailed; it is robbed of its natural, instinctive, spontaneous development. It cannot increase with the increase of God. There must be some concrete body in which it can put out those inner capacities with which it has been endowed for the kingdom hereafter in heaven.

And certainly that heavenly condition which belongs to its essence has evidently, according to S. Paul, already begun. Faith finds itself in possession already, in some degree, of the society, the household, the assembly, the body into which it has been translated. There has been a body, a society prepared for it, into which it has found itself inserted, introduced, from the first moment of its belief—"the Church, which is Christ's Body." Here, in this ordained system, in its ministries, sacraments, discipline, the soul is enabled to realize, to train, to foster, to practise those social characteristics which belong to its inherent and essential construction. Here, in this sacramental representation on earth of that holy society, of that heavenly Jerusalem, of that Divine Body of Christ now at the right hand of God, the soul could begin its exercise of those intricacies and relationships which are vital to its growth, and in which will, finally, consist its everlasting joy.

And in passing under these regulated ministries, in submitting to these forms of combination, it is not entering into novel, or additional, or artificial, or arbitrary, or temporary expediencies. Rather, it is arriving at itself; it is discovering its own character; it is realizing its own natural possibilities; it is fulfilling its own inherent necessities; it is feeling its limbs; it is evoking its gifts; it is testing its powers; it is facilitating its growth. By joints and bands, ministered, nourished, and knit, it is "making increase with the increase of God."

Faith and a Church, then, are correlative, not antithetical, terms. They imply and involve one another. To believe in Christ is to believe in a Church.

What, then, are we to say of those who differ and say, "We believe, but we see no necessity for incorporating our belief in any Church"? Are we to say, "This is not faith; there is no genuine faith in Jesus which does not include a Church"? Obviously, in the face of facts, this would be a ludicrous assertion. Faith there certainly is, deep, fervent, energetic; faith which puts to shame our lagging zeal, our worldly sloth, and which yet deems any Church system to be a mere accidental expedient and nothing more. No! But this we must say, this we cannot but say—that all genuine faith in Jesus Christ holds within it the secret, the germ of the Church; its inner construction anticipates a Church; its type, its form, its character, prepare it for insertion into a society, a body, a system, an order. Deprived of this, it must miss something of its perfect development; it cannot be attaining to all its proper fruit. Something is lost; something lies dormant and unused. There are gifts in it which are not exercised, and possibilities which remain unfulfilled. Strong and robust as this faith is, which we watch on all sides of us, we must think that it could not fail to become riper, richer, fairer, if it had behind it and around it the pressure and the might, so steady and so sure, of a continuous and unbroken body of disciplined forces and gathered resources, stored and garnered out of the accumulated experiences of a hundred Christian generations, exercised and put to profit under the weighty tradition and by the delicate discretion of an articulated and organized system, directed and filled by the ministerial Spirit of God, Who takes of Christ and distributes to each the gift, severally as He will, so framing and fashioning, by manifold offices under a single Lordship, the manifold Body of Christ. Here, surely, is what all personal faith needs and exacts. For this it cries aloud. Without this, it cannot but be crippled, narrowed, hampered. Such a system as this is no accidental expedient. It is the loss of it which is the accident—a mournful and heart-breaking accident, over which we must bow our heads in shame, and weep our penitential tears for the sins which have so hidden the blessed vision from our eyes.

And, surely, if we are right, if the inner character of faith makes for a Church, we have our comfort too ; for the day must come when this will show itself. This ardent, this tender faith, so living and so loving, which we watch with rueful eyes from our widowed obscurity, will be conscious of some want. It will have a sense of something incomplete ; it will miss its home ; it will yearn to fulfil itself in some larger whole ; it will be conscious of its hidden relationships, its inner sympathies, astir and at work ; it will feel abroad after some body to which, by construction, in secret it already belongs, and for whose uses it is already adapted. Where is it, it will ask, this something for which we are made—this home of faith, this corporate society, this organic kingdom ? Where can we discover it—an organization which can profess to reach from beginning to end, from Pentecost to the final Advent, and which can offer faith a means by which it can be knit up into that undivided work of God, which builds up, age after age, a single temple, and weaves, generation after generation, a single garment, the seamless robe, woven from the top throughout? Some day this solitary faith will look (we cannot but believe) for some such consummation. Where will it discover what it seeks?

Ah! beloved, what would be our joy if, when the good day comes, when the disclosure is made, when the secret is out—that secret which now lies at the root of all true faith, the secret of the Church—what joy, beyond all dreaming, if we might be able to run out from our retreats, holding in our hands our priceless treasure, and crying to them, "Here it is, the thing you need, that which you look for! Not for our own merits, but by God's great mercies, it is ours! In spite of our shame, in spite of our sin, behind all the clouds and obscurities of our doubtful career, this we still held fast; this we never wholly lost; to this, through long years of dark dismay, and just judgment, and deserved defeat, we yet desperately clung. We still possess it—this Apostolic order, this unbroken ministry, this continuous gift. The type, the form, the mechanism, the framework of the Body of Christ—this, at least, is ours to offer you. You bring us much that is strong and abundant; let this be our plea for pardon—that, faithless and faint-hearted, base and unkind, as we have often shown ourselves, we did not wholly fail our peculiar post; we did not throw away the one pearl that God had lodged in our hands; we held fast to it, at all hazards, and through days of bitter contempt; and here it is, at the hour when you need it, dimmed, perhaps, but not destroyed. Enough reward for all our pain, and more than enough, that now, when you feel the want of it, we are not wholly empty-handed; we have that to offer which, without us, you could not have in an English fashion, with a national tradition. Yes; the chance of forming a great English Church, united and whole, Catholic and Apostolic—this is still open to us all, is still possible. In the hope of this we held on to our heritage in hours when it looked useless and perverse. Now we can thank God that it was not for ourselves we held it, but for you."

This shall be our hope and prayer for them and for ourselves. And, in the mean time, what richness of spiritual life does this character of faith promise those who already understand its corporate nature, and enjoy its privileges! Such a faith is ever in growth; it "increaseth with the increase of God." For if we are "called in one body;" if our faith is an act of adherence, by which we receive admission within the system and kingdom of the redeemed, then it will in itself, in its very structure and composition, hold infinite suggestions of that kingdom to which it belongs, of that Body to which it adheres. In it, beneath it, above it, about it, that vast realm spreads and works, which reaches down from the very feet of the Father, until, at its outermost edge and fringe, it runs its lines round us, it embraces us—even us, so far, so tiny, so infinitely blessed! What inexhaustible delight there is in store for us, as day by day we learn, under ever new experiences, all the mystery that lay hidden in that first child-act of belief, which knit us into this immense and delicate fabric, which ministers to us and nourishes us, down all its rhythmic articulations, by that which every joint supplieth! Every year, every hour, there might be, if we were but alert, a fresh disclosure, a surprise, a discovery, of all that was involved within that original and wonderful entrance within the Body of Christ.

Yes, such a faith as this grows; and as it grows we shall see how and why a faith of this kind is bound to be intellectual, theological, dogmatic. For it is no spasm of emotion—vague, isolated, intermittent, abrupt; it is a definite and positive act, which plants us down in the thick of manifold conditions, relations, principles. Until we wilfully forfeit our place, there we abide—located, ingrafted, imbedded. A fixed body of laws plays through us and over us; an orderly system encompasses and feeds us. And now it is our part to apprehend, to unravel, all the wonder of the change. Slowly it all becomes clear; slowly, point by point, the great disclosure proceeds; slowly we can collect ourselves, and note, and examine. We begin to understand;

we grow into comprehension; we measure, we weigh, we ponder; we can distinguish some of the main laws and rules which govern the kingdom of the redeemed; we look up, by degrees, and down; we can faintly guess what it would be, with the saints, to comprehend the breadth, and length, and depth, and height, and to know the love that passeth all knowledge.

And all this intellectual work of apprehension springs still out of that original act of faith. It never leaves it; it issues from it; it is but spelling out the mystery which is already our life. Theology is but the slow unravelling of faith, the gradual and more accurate comprehension of the great system within which the soul is playing its new and strange part.

And such a theology must be dogmatic; it must make assertions which we cannot test; it must—for it reveals a system which spreads far, far away beyond our little ken. We can see and learn the laws that work within our own souls; and we can become perfectly sure that those same laws hold good throughout this immense kingdom—they are its one secret, its only key. Summarized in the Creed, they lie at the heart of the kingdom, and yet work even down to us at its uttermost fringe. That we can be sure of; but how they work elsewhere, and with what results—ah, how can we say! Suggestions, hints, glimpses, drawn from our own wonderful experiences—yes, these we have; but we know but a tiny corner, we see but a fragment. We can but guess the rest; we can but wait to know. We cannot cover it, cannot apprehend. No; but we can accept and believe the dogma, where it passes beyond our range, just because we have become certain, by our own native experience, of the verity and the power of that redemptive love of God in Christ, which has brought us into this kingdom of grace. Certain of that? We could die for that; and we know that it is that same love which holds this whole kingdom together, and which is supreme even there where we cannot follow its work, and are staggered, perhaps, by its results.

Why, then, should we be so restless, so anxious,

so disturbed? Be sure that what the life is at any one point in the Body, that same thing it must be at all. We know it, at one point; know its blessed gentleness, its unfailing goodness, its fathomless love. Why can we not trust it, there where it passes out of our sight? Surely we will rely upon it; we will accept; we will wait to know all in that great day, when all shall be made manifest!

Only one thing is necessary now: to know it, to understand it, to be sure of it, there where we can cover it, there where it is at hand, in our own souls. Ah, have we done that? Uncertain there, we shall be uncertain of all; but once certain there, we shall be quiet and at peace about the rest, waiting for the hour, the happy hour, when we shall know even as we are known.

And one word more. Such a faith is not only inherently dogmatic, but also inherently moral. And this, again, just because it is no lonely act. It plants us down amid that network of relationships by which the body is bonded and built; and these relationships constitute our moral obligations. Their appropriate actions and motions, made inevitable by the new situation—these are the virtues, the excellences of the kingdom of God. To correspond with our place and portion in the body, in harmonious contact with our fellows, this is the secret of the new character of Christ's citizens. That character roots itself therefore in faith; it issues out of our faith; it is the native and spontaneous activity of faith. For it is faith which holds the head; and, so holding, it must act and move so as to fulfil its part in the body, which is filled from end to end with Christ, and in which Christ is all in al

"Hold to the Head," then; believe in Christ, and the issue is inevitable Faith uncloses itself; it opens out into acts of virtue, into the fruits of the Spirit. This is the law of holiness; and it is in the recognition of this law that we escape all possible conception of any divorce between faith and moral conduct. If faith be, by its origin, "of the Body," corporate, social, then it is also, by its origin, ethical. As it opens out into corporate relationships, it opens out also into reciprocities, obligations, duties, correspondences, with their proper tempers, motives, excellences,—all of which constitute the holy character. Faith, by its very disclosure of its own inner essence, reveals itself as love. By exhibiting itself as the principle of adherence into a Body, it, by its very nature, takes upon itself a life prescribed and ordained. Faith, if it "holds to the Head," cannot but move, work, grow; cannot but be fruitful: cannot but "make increase with the increase of God." Is it because our faith is so private, so individual, that it is also so idle and so impotent?

THE PATTERN IN THE MOUNT.

"After that He through the Holy Ghost had given commandments unto the Apostles whom He had chosen."—ACTS i. 2.

It is impossible not to turn back, again and again, from the midst of our perplexities, to those great Forty Days, during which the mind of the Apostles passed from out of the confusion and littleness of its Gospel-period into the firmness and the width of the Epistles.

What were the impressions then implanted? What conception did they then receive from the Master, as He came and went, of the work before them; of the kingdom they were to establish, of the Church of which they should be the foundation? When they emerged out of that strange hidden time—emerged new men transformed, men on whom some wonderful experience had passed, which had broken up their old nature, and had lifted them on to a new level, from which they saw with other eyes than of old and spoke with other lips;—when they emerged, what were the ruling ideas which the power of the Risen Lord had stamped upon their imagination? What had they mainly gathered from Him as to the form and the features to which He desired that His Church on earth should, under their handling, correspond?

So we ask; and the answer is given in three or four metaphors, invariably occurring throughout the Apostolic writings, which most certainly convey the mind of the Lord about His Church, as His Apostles understood it. Three or four pictures He left stamped incradicably home. By these they were to work; here were their examples, their cue, "the pattern shown them in the mount." Let us recall these figures that were to them so familiar and so predominant; let us recall them, even though their very recollection clouds us with the sorrow of a passionate regret, which the Spirit of God alone can lighten. Let us recall them, at the risk of some repetition of what is already familiar to us, in order that we may, by bringing them together in one brief review, appreciate their weight and significance as a whole. They are the figures of the household, the family, the body, the temple.

First, the household. As He pictured to His heart that after-work, He certainly hoped and planned that all Christendom should take the form of a household whose master was gone for a time, but whose returning presence was to be the goal of all efforts and the sanction of all toil. This Christendom of His should be, pre-eminently, from one end to the other, an organized kingdom of work—work, busy, earnest, urgent, unflagging, as of a man entrusted with his goods by a master who looks eagerly for his profit, for his fruits; who delights in the man who can turn five talents into ten, and two into five. It was to be, in every corner of it, a busy home of progressive work, reaping interest, ever laying hold of fresh earthly matter and turning it into Divine uses. And as such a kingdom of business, nothing would be accidental, or fortuitous, or irregular. The household would bear the marks of plan, of deliberation; everywhere activity, nowhere disorder; everybody with an office, a function to fulfil; all united under a single system, prosecuting a single aim, moving under fixed rules and an orderly commission. That is what He would leave behind Him, this Master Who goes into a far country; and so He prayed that it should remain during the whole long time until He come again. All were to be found there, each at his post—the clerk at his desk, the servant in the kitchen, the porter at the door, watching and working on and on, with lamps trimmed, with loins girt, to the very moment when the Lord should be suddenly heard knocking at the gate.

So the Lord pictured His Church, in its busy work of incessant advance. And then, looking at it in its continuity, as conveying down the traditions and experiences of the past, He saw it all as "one family." "A family." An organized life of fixed and intelligible relationships; a life in which obligations lie deep within the very nature of those who are to fulfil them—obligations stringent and binding, outside all discussion. In the family, every separate life has worth; it must be considered; its interests, its wants, its character, all justify themselves by the mere act of existing. It is no matter of choice or consent, of likes or dislikes; for beyond all dispute the imperative claim holds good, " He is my brother, she is my sister—bone of my bone, flesh of my flesh." And this inherent necessity of kinship it is which gives such peace to family life—that peace which is so dear to us all in our home—the peace of feeling that nothing can override, or weaken, or destroy the moral bonds which knit its members together. It is in the very depth of the obligation that the secret of its joy lies. Born into us, it buries itself beyond the reckoning of reason; it penetrates our feelings; it fuses itself with our emotions; it imbeds itself within our instincts; it rounds our waking life with larger horizons. The family, the home—these lay nursing arms about us; they convey into our blood the strength and the fragrance of the past; they encompass us with warm and comfortable associations; and within this comfortable warmth the affections wake and stir, and sympathies come and go, and tenderness and gentleness put out their sweet powers, and under their kindling fosterage there spring up out of the heart the noise and bubble of happy laughter.

This is the home as we know it, and Christ would have His Christendom to be a home with the boons of home about it—the unquestioned security, the numberless and unbargained duties, fulfilled by the very instinct, undiscussed and undiscounted, as the natural doings of the day. No consent would have to be asked, no compact would intervene. To be a Christian—that shall be the only claim, which should be to us as imperative, as far beyond all argument, as, "That is my mother." Within this wide home of God, every soul would know itself at home; would go in and out freely, without question, without permission, in the full freedom of the Son. The habits, the associations, the language, the ways, all would be its very own

—its own, beyond all beginning, beyond all memory. Every separate soul would be given worth; his interest, his character, allowed for, recognized, justified. No lives would go wounded and unfellowed; no affection should be crushed and nipped; no blind collision, no bitter friction, no secret venom, no cruel ignorance, no unbrotherly contempt, would work their mischief in this home of peace; no blood would drip from secret gashes; but round every one would be the brightness of recognition, the warmth of companionship, the expansion, the gladness, the exultation, the laughter of home. So the Great Master, our Brother, thought, desired, schemed, figured; so they understood Him, those Twelve who broke bread with Him.

And how else did He picture His Christendom?

As a body—the familiar figure, which carries with it so much significance. Christendom, as the Master saw it, ought to be visibly and undeniably one thing from end to end, bounded by positive outlines, compact, concentrated, solid. It would not lie loose, weltering, vague, inorganic; but would be upgathered into a single whole, that would move altogether when it moved at all. One heart would beat within it, one food nourish it, one brain direct it, one interest absorb it. Throughout it all, communication would be open, penetrative, quick, unhindered; one joy would radiate, one sorrow becloud it; one soul would fill it, one speech break from its lips. Nor would there be any part within it that lacked its sustenance, for all would be in common.

And, so harmoniously formed, through it would pass unchecked the Glory of Him Who made it for Himself. God's mind, God's meaning, God's presence—these would be assured to all; for His Church would be to Him a body, an organ of visible expression, a medium of perfect communication. Christ would have a mouth to speak through, and hands to touch us, and feet wherewith to move abroad, and a voice by which to call. There would be no mistake where the risen Jesus was to be found. All who had eyes to see could tell where

He was, for He would possess a body upon earth, which would evidence and pledge His presence.

And in this thought we can pass to His last picture.

Christendom would be a temple—a place, visible, known, ordered, fixed, secure, where God could most certainly be found, met with, spoken to. The whole body of Christians would be as a sacred spot, hallowed and solemn—a building, lighted, fair, seemly, into which building faith would weld us, stone upon stone, each quarried, squared, selected, numbered; each laid close to each, dove-tailed and bonded, with quiet purpose, with distinct deliberation. No restless anxieties would shake and fret us, where we should go, what we are for; but the one steady hand of the Master Spirit would shape, carry, deposit each of us there and nowhere else, just where it were fitting. Ah! how happy to feel the blessed joinings closing in about us without jolt or hitch, and the mortar sealing us, and the wall growing up all round, and we laid there, each still and sure, knowing only that all is well with us! So it would rise, as some vast cathedral rose and grew in old days, with every century adding some new feature, some varied force, yet always one house, ever old and ever new.

The temple of God! That is what we were to be. No rough, unshapen mass; no unworthy and contemptible shelter; no stable full of unclean things; but a temple of God, strong and beautiful, sweet and pure, delicate in skill and rich with art, so that men might feel the power and awe of God's own splendour, might wake up and be sure "God is in this place. God is here, in these deep foundations, in these shining walls. Surely He is in this place, and we know it!" And then, within it, if any entered, the great worship would be ever proceeding, full of serious, honourable dignity, a worship, as of that temple in heaven, uniform, massive, continuous, complete; ever the moving priest, the uplifted hands, the eternal song, the rhythmic praise, the breath of Heaven, the powers of benediction, the motions and outgoings of grace.

So Christ our Master pictured it, desired it;

these were the visions that He showed His friends in the Mount. How can we bear even to remember them? How is it that our hearts can keep from breaking as we turn from the patterns shown us and look round on the Christendom which should have been all this, and which is what we know it, what we see it,—no beautiful temple, no fair body, no kindly home, no busy vineyard; but broken and shivered, loose and disarrayed. "The Lord hath broken down the hedge of His vineyard, so that all they that go by pluck off her grapes." "We are become an open strife to our neighbours, and our enemies laugh us to scorn." "The beast of the field devours it; the wild boar of the wood doth root it up." And we stand forlorn, impotent, hungry for fellowship, athirst for peace, and yet must gaze out in weary weakness, over dividing gulfs of "salt estranging sea," over sundering fissures cloven between brothers by the judgment of God, reaching out powerless hands to those with whom we shall never take sweet counsel, with whom we shall never walk together in the house of God as friends. Nay; for "Ephraim is evil to Judah, and Judah to Ephraim." Ah! so fatigued we are of our warrings; and yet, when our hearts burn, and we long to run across to those far off and throw our arms about their necks, then the strong hands hold us back; hard wrongs and ancient sins all intervene; the way is barred. Sick at soul, we turn back to our darkened house! What may be done? What is possible? Wherein lies our faithfulness to the vision that the Master showed us?

First, and above all, we have to be loyal to the facts. Nothing comes out more wonderfully to those who ponder on the ways of God than His patient conformity to the actual situation into which men have brought themselves. Even when the conduct of men drags the Divine work itself into difficulty, when it thwarts and curtails God's own schemes, still God follows men along the way they have chosen; still He finds means not to desert them; still He keeps close at their side. The only thing He can never bring Himself to do is to forsake them. If they will not allow Him their best, He will do what He can with their worst. He will adapt Himself to the conditions they force upon Him; He will, at any cost to Himself, work through human materials. Never will He commit violence to nature; never, until all is lost, will He sweep obstacles aside by some avenging flood. Close to facts He ever clings, building through them, fashioning them, so that He may win them over to His cause. If not in this way, then in that. He has a thousand methods; He has infinite resources; His arm never wavers, but His mercy waits upon all the shifts and shocks of human circumstance.

This is the story, the secret, of His revelation in the Bible. It is historical; it uses all the motions and changes of our history—that strange, mixed, uncertain history, crossed by blind currents of sin, and swayed hither and thither by buffeting winds of error. He uses that disturbed and fluctuating movement as the scene of His display, as the instrument of His Divine disclosure. Point by point He follows it, as it swings hither and thither. No conditions are too surprising for Him to manipulate; no obstinacy of men so obstructive that He will lose heart with it. All down that Jewish story we watch Him, adopting as His own all the melancholy fate to which their wilful guilt reduces them. They fall, they lapse, they blunder into wrong paths, they shatter His hope, they despise His leading; and still, as their ruin scatters them beyond Damascus and beyond Babylon, He is there, traveling with them into sad exile, far from the haggard and wasted halls of Zion. God is there with them, still discovering new means, under the shadows of the Captivity, by which to recover His own, by which to rebuild their broken fortunes, by which to win new omens of His Christ. Still He is there, weaving out of the very loneliness of Babylon's waters new and tenderer songs wherewith to greet the coming Lord. Still ever He is there at their side; still, under the cloud, pursuing the one indomitable hope.

That is our God! In that long story we can

read His heart. Far, far from Him the dead immobility which we so lightly ascribe to omnipotence, the rigid adherence to an unelastic and unyielding ideal. Far, far from Him the petulance of the artist, of the enthusiast, of the idealist, who cannot tolerate the rough defeats, the heart-breaking delays of actual life, nor can afford to bend to the stiff and coarse exigencies of material facts. Far from Him the human insistence on abstract perfection or nothing. His omnipotence shows itself in the inexhaustible pliability with which it will burrow under the facts, just as they stand, and lift them out of their degradation ; it is measured by the very depth to which it sinks its forces down within and below them. How strange to Him the temper we know so well, which violently thrusts some high ideal, neck and crop, into the thick of facts, and insists on absolute and immediate conformity to rule and line ; that temper which turns out, helter-skelter, all that fails to correspond to what the first principles demand ! How strange to Him the rapid logic which deduces, by syllogism, the exact course which God's perfection and omnipotence are bound to follow, the shape which His revelation or His Church are of necessity forced to take by the laws of His being! To hear men talk and argue, with swift, easy precision, from the premiss of God's omnipotence, one would suppose that the Bible had never been written—written as it is to tell us such a different story; to tell us that God's revelation will, at all costs, be historical; that is, it will never plunge an ideal scheme down, regardless of conditions, and then drag facts by violence into conformity with it; but will accompany man's movements, and defects, and collapses, and needs, and by means of them, with ever-living omnipotence, will work out the redemption that was born into us in Christ.

That redemption, indeed, is ever His sole instrument—"Christ the same, yesterday, and to-day, and for ever;" and, more than that, the methods or modes by which that redemption was and is intended to reach and touch us—these we know, these we have been considering under the guidance of Christ's own selected metaphors. In these we can see His intention; we can be quite sure of the type on which He framed His Church, and of the desire with which He shaped its order and its ministry.

And we who so see, we who can be certain that He endowed His believers with a fixed type of structure by which they could be welded into a single constitution—a house, a family, a body, a temple—we shall passionately value all that in His mercy still enables us to fulfil His own desire. Woe to us if we lightly abandon anything that belongs to that Divine intention. No! To all that retains the native elements of unity, to all that can make the recovery of lost unity possible, we shall cling with unfaltering grasp. To secure this, our priests may well endure imprisonment.

But while so doing we will not shut our eyes to all that has happened; we will not talk as if the whole situation were perfectly clear, precise, and intelligible; we will not attempt to tie up the resources of God in short, sharp, scrappy definitions; nor expect, amid the confusions which human sins have worked within Christ's Church, that all the outlines of the temple can stand out fine-edged, four-square, and all the paths of grace be summed up in some glib phrase or easy formula. We will not attempt to define with accuracy the qualifications and modifications by which the Lord, Who by all means would save some, may be relieving the present distress. No; nor will we go on asserting that the ideal must exist in its complete perfection, in spite of all that man can do to disfigure it, and so asserting cut off all that interrupts or disturbs it, until we have saved the ideal at the cost of losing all the material that it was intended to cover and to redeem,—at the cost of ignoring all the facts of history and of life which clamour for consideration. Nor will we, again, because God's Church is intended to be united and complete, rush over and hide ourselves within its largest fragment, trusting that its very size may help us to forget that it is but a fragment after all.

We will be true to the mind of Christ, and we will be true to the teaching of undeniable fact;

and where the two seem to collide, we have the word of prophecy.

Prophecy! Is it not just the help that we need? Prophecy, which beholds the vision, which looks for its definite realization, and yet sees it deferred, hampered, thwarted again and again by the cruelty of facts; and yet is sure of its hope, and yet asserts that (be the facts what they may) nevertheless the vision is not lost or falsified. Its powers are still with us; its possibilities are all preserved; the remnant, the holy seed, is guarded and saved, as the life within the withered trunk. The organic life may shrink, may lie almost hidden; but it is there. The germ is transmitted, the tradition preserved, the deposit retained; it can open out again when the good day comes. God guards the holy seed within His Church; and while that is guarded, all may be restored. We may all come again to Zion with songs and everlasting joy upon our heads; we may yet feed our flocks in beautiful security upon the slopes of Carmel and of Bashan, as in the blessed days of old.

Let us have comfort. God's resources are infinite. He has many methods. If the house, the temple, the body be hindered and held back from their completeness, then He has other metaphors by which He foretold the nature of His kingdom. It would not only come in lovely and visible beauty, as a bride adorned for the marriage, but also it would work as leaven buried in the lump—a shapeless, seething ferment amid blind, obstructive matter. It would come as a mustard seed, hidden where no eye saw, a small and disregarded atom, growing as a seed in the night while men slept. It would be as a field full of tares. It would be as a treasure buried in a field, which, for long years, a man might walk over and know nothing of, until the day at last comes when he discovers what had been there all along, and he lets everything else go that he may secure that field.

Here are indications and suggestions for our comfort. The kingdom of God has many modes of entry among us. If we choke the finer and cleaner passages, God is patient enough to work by the rougher and less shapely methods. For He has taken upon Him our infirmities. His perfection does not shrink from co-operating with our imperfection. He waits upon our weakness. He "has undertaken to deliver man," and at all risks He will achieve it. He will "not abhor the Virgin's womb;" He will refuse nothing that is necessary to that original resolution. Our humble part is plain enough. It is for us to hold fast to principles wherever we see them, and to leave to God the problem of their realization, of their fulfilment, neither asking nor attempting to answer questions beyond our measure, but content to guard what is given, and confident in prophetic hope that what He has promised He will in His own good time perform.

Two pledges, two securities, are always ours. First, there is the present existence of grace, to be received and taken into our individual lives, sufcient for the day, felt in its undoubted power upon our souls, coming, feeding, carrying, strengthening, with its unfailing message of peace, "It is I; be not afraid." Christ comes to us; Christ is with us in the boat; His touch assures us; His hand controls. Trust this, use this, and wait and hope!

And, secondly, so using, so trusting, and with access assured, pray for the recovery of that completeness which you know that He desires. Pray for the full order and unity for which He prayed His own last prayer. Pray, in the knowledge of His mind, for the blessing of the family, the solidity of the body, the beauty of the temple, in the light of the vision, according to the pattern shown you. "Pray for the peace of Jerusalem." Pray for the vine in its fulness, as He planted it, when "He prepared room for it, and it took root and filled the land; when the hills were covered with the shadow of it, and the boughs thereof were like the goodly cedar trees; when she sent out her boughs unto the sea and her branches unto the river." Pray and plead with Him, "O Lord, how long wilt Thou be angry with Thy people that prayeth? Why hast Thou, then, broken down their hope?" Pray, believing in your heart that all may yet be restored. "Return, we beseech Thee, O Lord of hosts. Look down from heaven; behold and visit this vine, and the place of the vineyard which Thy right hand hath planted, and the branch that Thou madest so strong for Thy own self." Pray that He Who still sitteth between the Cherubim may, "before Ephraim, Benjamin, and Manasses, stir up His strength and come and help us." Yea, "Turn us again, O Lord God of Hosts; shew us the light of Thy countenance, and we shall be whole."

OUR CITIZENSHIP.

"For the edifying of the Body of Christ."—EPHES. iv. 12.

As soon as spirit touches spirit there springs up between them a relationship, which we call moral. Whatever rightly follows from such spiritual contact is morally good; what we mean by goodness is the issue, the outcome, the inevitable activity, which is bound to follow from the nature of spirits, whenever the contact between them is free, true, and pure. Moral goodness, therefore, shows itself under the conditions of companionship; contact is essential to its manifestation.

So it is in the intercourse of human society (as we know) that man proves himself to be a moral being; as soon as he associates himself with others, moral obligations, of necessity, discover themselves.

His efforts to correspond to the conditions of the family and of the city reveal the lines of the natural virtues as their spontaneous outcome.

And therefore it is that faith, by admitting us into fresh contact with God and with our fellows; by endowing us with new relationships that have become ours through our inclusion within the new humanity within the Body of Christ, has necessarily laid upon us new moral obligations, responsibilities, functions, all which spring out of the very nature of our corporate faith. We are brought into a new family, a new city, of higher origin and of purer ties; we stand amid a web of supernatural communications, to which we are forced to respond in some way or other. We walk in the New Jerusalem; there lies our citizenship; and therefore new habits and a new behaviour are of necessity demanded of us—demanded by the commandment of love, which is new, since it has knit us one with another by utterly new joints and bands; and yet is old, for it is the same love, under higher conditions, which bound us into families and cities by

the sweet ties of the natural virtues in the homes of earth.

If, then, we would seek to determine the features and lines of the Christian temper and character, we must look to the nature of this great fellowship into which we have been called. The Christian character asked of us is that habit, that activity, which must follow on our acceptance within the assembly of the firstborn, within the city of God. Whatever that acceptance makes desirable, makes natural, that is good, that is holy. So acting, we walk in the light; we exercise our citizenship; we are built into the Body; we edify the Church.

The Church, then, is no formal mechanism; it is a moral conception, a moral condition, by which we are to determine character. And, in fact, it is only within the borders of a Church that any serious attempt has been made at a full and complete treatment of the Christian character. I would ask you, therefore, to take those four great symbols which, as we said, embodied, to our Lord and His Apostles, the type of the united Church, and consider what is the moral character which they would need and foster.

It will be something, surely, if, amid the clouds that obscure and baffle those deep unities of our spiritual society, we can nourish within our own lives the seeds and germs of that peculiar character which nothing but a Church can breed, because nothing but the conception of a Church makes it desirable. So labouring, we shall, at least, be removing that within ourselves which obstructs the union of believers into a single fellowship.

Each symbol, if we consider, suggests its own peculiar and appropriate excellence of character. Let us take the Church as a household. What are the virtues essential to a household such as our Lord pictured, to an organized kingdom of work? First, fertile activity. The moment we recall that house of business, we see that the character fit for it will certainly not be immersed in self, in broodings, in morbid and melancholy musings, in idle dreams. All these must disappear from the soul set to work there. Its chief occupation is not in its own part, in its own trials and sorrows; its eyes are not imprisoned within the story of its own salvation. It must be up and doing; it must look ahead. "Thou hast saved us, O my Father; blessed be Thy Name! Now, what dost Thou need of me? Though I have been, indeed, a man of unclean lips, yet Thou hast touched me with the live coal from off Thine altar; and now I have but one desire, one passion—Here am I; send me!" Such a character, so inspired, will be forthcoming, energetic, stirring; it will be strong for action; it will have nerve and fibre, bone and substance; it will show mastery; it will contribute force.

Is, then, the Christian character, as we know it, a thing of this kind? Is energy, is force always its characteristic? Alas! we are weak, it may be, through old sins and wrongs; we cannot be active, masterful, and keen. No; and if so, Christ has all His compassions open; but, nevertheless, He will have much to forgive in us. We will recognize and confess it. So far as we are weak, poor, moody, stupid, dull, we are below what He wants. We will not, then, flatter ourselves over our own melancholies, our sensitive depressions, our nerveless poverty of spirit. We will not interest ourselves in these inactive and impotent miseries. We will remember that the cardinal sin charged against the members of His Church by Christ is the sin of which we take so little account and so lightly excuse—sloth, spiritual sloth ; the Church's sin ; the sin of the house, which is, above all things, to keep watch and ward for the returning Master ; the sin of that wicked servant who hides his gift in a napkin ; the sin of the steward who says, " My lord delayeth his coming ;" the sin of the unlit lamp and the ungirt loin; the sin of spiritual thoughtlessness, against which the awful judgment delivers its relentless message, " Too late, too late ; ye cannot enter now."

The household demands activity of character, and it asks also for a skilled and trained activity. An organized kingdom of work must have perfected, disciplined instruments, allotted to particular functions and trained into intelligent skilfulness. Life—the Christian life—is not to be a mere rough-and-tumble affair, justified by the raw and boisterous heartiness of its belief. It is to be a fine and delicate adaptation to a definite work; it is to be a real business, requiring apprenticeship, and watchfulness, and gradual attainment; a thing of audits, and reckonings, and careful notes; of forethought, prudence, patience, as of clerks handling an ordered and intricate commerce, with rules, and seasons, and enterprises, and slow profits, and calculated returns. The Christian character will have about it the marks of a wise and growing experience, trained in view of practical purposes of its own—trained to handle spiritual matters with ready and beautiful ease. Ah, how the words rebuke us! When the spiritual kingdom draws near, calls upon us to speak, act for it, give evidence, carry its message, are we not surprised and distressed at our own awkwardness, our unreadiness, our uncouth efforts, our ungainly speech, so hesitating, so unpractised, so inadequate? How rare—ah, how wofully rare!—to see on the earth one of whom we can say, "Look! There is something as perfect in its own exquisite way as the skill of an expert or an artist, among the children of this world. There is the flawless work of grace; there is a finished and chastened Christian character. Look! in the things of God, how quick his insight, how delicious his free motion, how true his touch; how responsive and keen and alive is all his lifeforce; how rich and entire its dedication to Divine uses, its familiarity with Divine things!"

Trained and masterful skill; that is the fruit of the household. And the family—what type, what rule of character will it suggest? The family, on earth, is the very home of virtues; and Christ, in declaring this new society to have about it the ties and familiarities of a family, constitutes it a nursery and school of character. There, in the family of God, the character of each believer is given a background. That character is to be no upstart growth of a day; it is no flash or fling of wilful self-assertion; it is no piece of individual vigour, audacious and personal; not shot out of a pistol, full of accidental whims and vagaries. These all drop away from a character that is bred within the close companionship of a family—a family with continuous traditions, with memories of honour, with an inherited wealth of rich and fine experiences, with accumulated responsibilities, with a tone and a temper into which has passed the mellow fragrance of ancient dignities. A family breeds a character of courtesy; a delicate sense of others' rights, interests, worth; a sensitive recognition of varying characteristics, gifts, degrees, types, functions, feelings. It instils self-repression, self-control, the honour for one another, the esteem of one another, the stooping of the strong to the weak, the absence of all loud and clamorous glorying, the reverence which cannot trample on others, nor ride roughshod over their scruples or their sentiments.

And in the family, again, this negative self-repression will learn to give itself positive and active outflow, in sympathy, tenderness, affection; it will be ready at another's call, quick to share another's sorrow, or, what is harder, perhaps, to kindle at another's joy. It will watch how to help in secret, giving little lifts to burdens, unknown and unthanked, foregoing its own wants, forgetting its own cares, with that instinctive helpfulness which only affection can prompt and only unselfishness can discover. Alas! is this the sure type of character in every Christian? Do we always find this, where we find belief in Christ's Church? Is it not too possible for strong belief itself to harden our sensibilities; to give us a crushing self-confidence, a self-assertive intolerance, from which tender souls shrink as if wounded? Cannot our very faith sometimes induce us to take an acute interest in ourselves; to be greatly occupied with its story, its interests, its peculiarities, until we pride ourselves on just that in it which is most personal to us and therefore least valuable—until we cannot credit or endure other roads by which belief has been reached, nor appreciate the infinite and exquisite diversity of characters which are all, by manifold graces, drawn together into the family of God, wherein there should be "neither Jew nor Greek, neither barbarian nor Scythian, neither male nor female"?

Let us ask ourselves whether we have ever begun the education of the Christian family; whether our faith in Christ has yet taught us, at all, to give increased worth to the lives about us; whether it has taken our attention off ourselves, and turned it upon the needs and hopes of others; whether it has made other people's lives more interesting to us; whether we have won a new patience and courtesy, a new respect for the weak, the uninteresting, the stupid, the wearisome, the depressed; whether it has bred in us the desire to honour all, to love the brotherhood—not those whom we select and like, but the whole Christian brotherhood as such—to esteem others better than ourselves; to give place to others; to wait upon others' cares? Has faith enlarged our stock of sympathy, quickened our affectionateness, softened our hardness, purged our wilfulness, rounded our angularities?

Has it? If not, we have forgotten that Christ founded a family of faith.

And the body—what stamp does this great conception set upon character? It, of course, carries yet further than the family the rule of limitation, of subordination, and all the moral excellences that result from this; but it adds a peculiar note—the note of witness. A body is, in essence, the evidence the proof, the pledge of that which acts through it. Its sole function, throughout all its parts, is to make manifest the secret presence which animates and directs it. It brings that presence out into act, into evidence; it makes it known. The Christian, who is "of the Body," has his mission, his vocation. He is sent; he is there to declare the Name, to manifest the glory, of God; to give evidence abroad of the God within.

The Christian believer must, then, be stamped with the seal of mission; he will move about his work, not only busy and keen, but as conscious of a message to be delivered throughout that work. Always he will be murmuring to himself, "Now we are ambassadors in the name of God." He is prophetic; he is, by the very life he lives, to make intelligible God's secrets, to unclose his mind towards men. He is a preacher in his acts; they are his sermon. By the great rule of our Lord, he will let his light so shine that men, as they see his good deeds, will glorify—not him; no, he will not suffer them to make that mistake. It will be too obvious that it is not his own doing; he will give his evidence too clearly for that. No; the spectators will instinctively and of necessity detect the source of his light, and will "glorify the Father, Who is in heaven." We are so to do our good works that men will not glorify us, but God. That is the task set us as members of Christ's Body; that is to be the note of our character. The hardest, highest law; for what a passion of self-repression will it not require, if ever it is to come to pass that, as we advance in holiness, we shall advance in humility, and that the more our light shines, blessing and gladdening those about us, the more directly and immediately men may turn their eyes off us, and may recognize that we are nothing and that God is all in all.

Dearly beloved, if this is the excellence peculiar to the body, what is the sin peculiar to the body? Hypocrisy; the acting of a part, the pretence to do, of ourselves, that which is done in and through us by God. "Woe unto you, scribes and Pharisees, hypocrites!" Hypocrisy; the sin of the body, of the flesh; the sin of resting the eyes, the attention, on self; on the tool, forgetting the workman; on the creature, forgetting the Creator. And this in the case of one's self; to suppose one's self the author of what one does, to thrust one's self into the place of God. Hypocrisy: to do this, not in pretence, to deceive others, entrap others' admiration—but to do it so that one beguiles one's self, flatters one's self, caresses one's self, admires one's self; and to do this, again, not in mere human affairs, but in the things of God, in the affairs of the kingdom, in the deeds of that Body of Christ into which God's mercy has placed us that we might do exactly the opposite—might glorify Christ, might declare the Name of God, might impel men to remember and recognize their Father Which is in heaven. Hypocrisy ; the sin of the devout, their own peculiar sin ; the sin built up out of the conditions of the religious life, as a cancer sucks its venomous sustenance out of our health ; the sin that develops its range and depth according to the measure and subtlety of the devotion on which it feeds, ever climbing higher as the religious aspiration moves upward ; the sin of Churchmen, of the painstaking, and continuous, and growing, and definite, and complete life of piety ; the sin which blots out the way of cure, and kills out the germs of salvation, and blinds, and hardens, and deadens, and freezes, and withers, and slays ; the sin loaded with such terrible judgment by the mouth of Him Who to sinners was so kind and merciful and tender.

Ah! what of this sin in ourselves? The world detects it so easily and condemns it so unsparingly. Why? Because it is a sin of which it is not capable, to which it cannot be tempted.

The godly alone are tempted. Men must be in earnest, men must be devout, to be capable of it at all. Churchmen are open to it, capable of it, with special ease; for the more complete and careful the rules of piety professed, the more liable we become to its miserable perversion; the higher the aim, the greater the risk. If you and I are seriously attempting to live as in the Body of Christ, then we have an ever-new peril to face; we have to keep a yet more delicate and rigid watch over our inward character, if men who see our good works are to glorify, at the sight, our Father Which is in heaven.

The character of the household—vigorous, skilful, fertile; the character of the family—restrained, courteous, tender; the character of the body—a character of vocation, void of all self-aim and self-pleasing, whose most instinctive actions make God visible, intelligible, evident, to men. These are some notes of our Church-character, our citizenship; and to these there is to be added the crown, the flower, the glory—the character of the temple.

The temple. There is to be positive beauty in

the Christian character; it is to be full of delicate and lovely refinement; there is to be a touch upon it of grace, charm, majesty, consecration. It pictures a life in which we shall be past the turmoil and the struggle; not always battling; not always scarred; not always faint, weary, broken; not always weeping, stumbling, falling. This must, indeed, come first—this wrestle, this night of toil, this bitter purging; it must be endured. But, after all, there is in us the power to come out into the light, and the sun, and the joy. Already, even on earth, the power of Christ's victorious cry, "It is finished!" will touch us with some breath of benediction. The struggle will begin to ebb, to fall back; the promise will be upon us of that day, when the morning will indeed break, and for us, too, all the Passion and the Cross will be finished and done. Yes, now and again, if we be faithful, the fierceness will slacken, the black sin will relax its grip, and there will spring up in us the sweet desires which make purity a joy and holiness a peace. Out of the heart will proceed no more the ancient horrors; but there will bud upward, like flowers, the spontaneous gifts of the Spirit, " love, gentleness, goodness, loving-kindness, faith, meekness, charity "—the graces of the high home in heaven. And then we shall know at last, or dimly feel, what it is to be of the temple of God, a stone in the chosen place where God abides, because He hath a delight therein—to be as a green olive-tree planted in the house of the Lord.

In the temple; fit for the temple! In such a life there would, above all, be perfect cleanness. The vessels of the Lord are all pure. He that ascends unto the hill must have clean hands, pure heart, an incorrupt life. The first necessity of a temple is, as Nehemiah knew, to be purged of all defiling traffic, of "them that sell fish." And more. Not only the coarse, gross things, but the very suspicion of the unclean thing, the very scent and taint of the world, must be wholly gone. Not enough just to be decent; just not to be unworthy; just to avoid blame; just to escape past sin. Nay; something excellent, something beautiful, something free and pure, is wanted for the temple—a life of love, which is jealous for God's honour, and is devoured with heat when that temple of God suffers dishonour; the love which is not afraid of the small cords and the discipline, if they be needed to purify God's house; the love which goes beyond the bare command, the naked necessities; the love which pours out its undemanded treasure, and bathes the Lord's feet with tears, though He be uninsistent, and ceases not to cover them with kisses, even though He has never asked for them. This is the love which alone can build up the character of the temple.

And such a character, so built up out of purity and love, will have about it also the sense of mystery —the mystery of the temple; the awe that hangs about those spots where the heights and the depths of God meet and mingle; the mystery of the vision, of the consecration; the mystery of the oil that ran down over Aaron; the mystery of the Mount of Transfiguration—that Mount where faces shine with strange exaltation, and the very garments are flooded with unearthly whiteness, and there are voices, and visitants, and unutterable things, whether in the body or out of the body, God knows! we cannot tell.

This purity, this mystery, the temple gifts—where are they to be found? Where are they, in our lives, so mixed, so unpurged, so worldly? How flat and shallow we all seem! How little wonder, mysteriousness, depth, there is felt about us! Does any one, sleeping in sin, wake ever, at our touch and presence, to a sense of Angels that are moving up and down the golden ladder, between heaven and earth? Does any one suspect us of secrets beyond his ken? Is any one ever awed into shame by our neighbourhood? Is there anything solemn, strange, holy, about us? Alas! all this is very far from most of us, we know too well. And we may well expect men to be unwilling to believe in a Church if we so rarely show them its moral and spiritual fruits. Not until we are more evidently of the body and of the temple will men be enabled to recognize and confess, "This is the generation of them that seek Thee, even of them that seek Thy face, O Jacob."

THE BUILDING OF THE SPIRIT.

" The Lord sitteth above the water-flood : and the Lord remaineth a King for ever."—Ps. xxix. 10.

As we watch in spring-time the returning swallows, and delight at the ever-new wonder of their flight, flashing, darting, wheeling, skimming along the startled waters, which they seem to laugh at as they touch and fan ; or, again, when we are shown the delicate and airy bone-work by which all this miracle of motion is made possible—which of us remembers all the toil, and pain, and pressure which lie around and behind that exquisite mechanism, that rapid ease ? Who can guess what rough warfare, what haunting fears, have gone to the perfecting of that fairy fabric ; what fierce foes it has used that victorious flight to escape ; what arduous effort after food is still at work preserving its swift symmetry ?

It is the same (as we now know) with all this bright and beautiful nature on which we feast our eyes as the sweet summer slowly steals over field and wood. We are watching a late result, of which the long history is hidden. The very beauty screens the secret from us. But as we push our way behind that screen, as we spell out its inner story, we learn what strange and troubled forces, what stormy scenes, have all gone to the making of that earth which now, in its completed triumph, smiles up at us, as a face at ease that is glad to feel itself alive and very fair.

Or we look out from some bridge over London at some hour—

> "When the city doth like a garment wear
> The beauty of the morning."

There it is, still as a dream, glorious as a vision, so secure, so steady, so quiet, at such peace

> "The river glideth at its own sweet will;
> Dear God, the very houses are asleep,
> And all this mighty heart is lying still."

Yes; there is embodied a victory, there is enshrined

and sealed a hope, a glory. "Towers, domes, pinnacles," all speak of a wonder that has come about—the wonder of human intercourse, human co-operation, human sympathy, by which new possibilities have opened, new hopes dawned, new splendours been achieved, far beyond the limits within which man first found his narrow lot cast when he wandered hither and thither, loose, savage, suspicious, and alone. There it lies, under our eyes. So far the riddle has been read, the vision has come true. Each tower, each spire, is a record and a pledge of a stage won, of a gain stored and secured.

But ah, at what a cost of blood and pain does that wide city sleep and dream in the clear morning air! What ages of suffering have passed in tumult and tempest before men could win their way up, out of distrust and alarm, into the confidence and peace of which these towers are the visible evidence! What noise and heat; what fever and fret; what anxieties, and perils, and wars; what dismal failures, and lapses, and stumblings, and falls; what painful recoveries; what bitter experiences; what miserable castigations; what wearisome delays; what stress and strain; what tyrannies, what crimes, what anarchies, have all gone to the shaping of this social order, which now assumes the comfortable air of a natural law, which no sane man can ever question or discuss! All this is thrown out of sight as we gaze, just as the quiet and untroubled face of a flower makes us forget the fears that beset its sowing amid the disgraces of winter skies.

And we who believe in Christ to-day are in danger of a like forgetfulness. We hold, for instance, in our hands the three great Catholic Creeds, the wonderful work of that Spirit Who fell upon the Church at Pentecost. To those of us who have been allowed to know their significance and their power, how strong and fair they seem, how steady their outlines, how unfailing their peace! We feed on their secure phrases, on their pregnant thoughts. Our hearts tingle to their mighty music, to their measured roll. With what freedom can we surrender ourselves to the onward movement of their high chanting: " I believe in Jesus Christ, the only-begotten Son of God, Begotten of His Father before all worlds, God of God, Light of Light, Very God of Very God, Begotten, not made, Being of one substance with the Father; By Whom all things were made. . . . And I believe in the Holy Ghost, the Lord and Giver of life, Who proceedeth from the Father and the Son, Who with the Father and the Son together is worshipped and glorified, Who spake by the Prophets." There is security; there is vigour; there is assurance; there is clear insight; there is the power of the Word, the infallibility of the Holy Spirit. So calm, so steady; such peace, such majesty. Far away, it seems, from all the dust of quarrel, from all the turmoil of dispute, from all the agony of indecision; far above the fretting and the fever. We are lifted into some great height of vantage; we, too, see with clear eyes; we, too, wear, like a garment, " the beauty of the morning."

Yet, how was that peace won? What lies behind

those strong words of faith? Were they enacted with that quiet ease with which they speak to us to-day? Were they struck out at one creative blow by the Spirit of God? Ah! we know well how strange, and long, and anxious, and bewildering was the process of which those Creeds are the fruit. Four centuries of almost unbroken trouble, perplexity, confusion, fear, dismay, have gone to their shaping; from the hour, the awful hour, when S. Paul wandered, distracted with evil rumours, up and down the borders of Macedonia, waiting for Titus to bring him news from rebellious and defiled Corinth, with fightings without, with fears within, with the sentence of death smiting him, not knowing whether his entire work were not about to be broken into ruins under his very eyes; on through all the fierce agonies which shook to its foundations the Apostolic Church, agonies which have left record after record throughout the latter books of the Bible, in passionate appeals to believers to hold fast the faith, to avoid " profane babblings and old wives' fables," to contend earnestly for the faith once delivered, because there are men crept in unawares, "ungodly men, turning the grace of God into lasciviousness, denying the only Lord God and our Lord Jesus Christ." There, and in many such another passage, we touch it—the blinding storm that swept down. There you can listen to the roar of the driving winds; you can feel the weight of the flood that beat against the walls of the house of faith until it shuddered. Those that came through that storm, those who still held true, must again and again, in moments of desperate need, have looked in each other's faces to ask, "Will this fury ever cease? Will the rock indeed hold out? Have we any footing? Who can endure to the end?"

Or, again, in the passionate cries of Ignatius, as he passes to his doom in Rome, we have something by which to measure the maze of bewilderment and peril that drew from him those words of flame —words that sting and bite, as, with beseechings that are wrung out of his heart's blood, he struggles to assert and secure the full reality of Christ's human nature.

And how can we describe the critical years that surround the four Great Councils, the years of which our actual Creeds are the direct fruit? As we run lightly over the story in our brief summaries of ecclesiastical history, the long intervals all drop out, the accidents and inequalities of the time disappear, and it all reads to us as if, the moment a heretic appeared, he was recognized at once, and his heresy noted, confuted, unmasked : whenever there was a perplexity the Church assembled in General Council and relieved all doubt by an authoritative declaration of what it was essential to believe. Could any description be less like what really occurred? No such simple clockwork machinery turned out a dogma whenever it was wanted. No such easy process saved or spared those Christians of the fourth century the pain and the distress which we sometimes fancy to be our own peculiar trial. For them there were long, long years between Nicæa, 325, and Chalcedon, in 451, in which no one knew which way to look for guidance and decision. The authorities themselves again and again spoke with contradictory voices. Good men were trapped into acquiescence; holy men, without sufficient speculative acumen to know where they were being led, lent their weight to false statements. And then the real question was encumbered by blunders, mischances, accidents. It got mixed up with side issues; it took years before it could be disentangled from compromises, and circumlocutions, and misdirections, and could be brought into that exact shape in which a real decision could become possible. And then there were complications from external influences: the intrigues of courtiers, the wilfulness of princes, the violence of mobs,—all these played their part, agitated the surface of affairs, disturbed and distorted the spiritual interests. The issue again and again seemed to hang on precarious accidents, on the lives of favourites, on the incalculable whims of ministers and empresses. And the normal ecclesiastical authorities were swept this way and that by the strong forces at work, and failed to give stable judgments. Bishops temporized, overcome, says S. Gregory, "by fear, or interest, or flattery, or, what is most excusable, by ignorance." Councils met and parted in bitter strife, or gave doubtful and suspicious verdicts, or passed ambiguous formulas that avoided the question at stake. Bishops stood over against Bishops and Churches against Churches. At times "the whole world groaned and wondered to find itself Arian," until at last the true faith, as we now so easily see it to have been, was housed in the clear head and the dauntless heart of a single champion, alone against the world; and he was flying in perilous exile from threats which daily menaced his life, condemned and expelled by large Councils of the Church at Antioch, Tyre, Arles, Milan, supported, in his heroic hour, by a laity more faithful than its pastors or its Popes.

For Popes failed. One yielded to the depression of a prison, and signed a compromising Creed. Papal delegates subscribed to the condemnation of Athanasius. Now, and again, some Pope was beguiled into favouring a doctrine which the sharper eyes of theological experts detected and denounced.

So the weary war rose and fell, with clamour and confusion, year after year. "We determine Creeds by the year," says S. Hilary, "or by the month; and then we change our determination; and then we prohibit our changes; and then we anathematize our prohibitions." And laymen were discussing seriously among themselves how to steer a straight path of belief through rival claimants, all of whom claimed to be orthodox and scriptural; and were conceiving the possibility of all living authorities being caught in temporary error; and were devising tests and standards, careful and laborious, by which the individual believer could still hope to hold fast the ancient form of sound words. And in the mean time the trouble darkens in ways so familiar to us. Devout and holy men, belonging to Arian or Nestorian Churches, were consecrating themselves to missionary enterprise, and were converting entire nations of incoming barbarians, innocent and unsuspecting, to a form of faith which the Church was forced to repudiate. And, again, passionate supporters of orthodoxy were falling over, in the blindness of zeal, into statements as unsteady and as deadly as those which they were so loyally opposing; and Athanasius has to repudiate his friends, and the Church to set itself against the foremost monks of Egypt, who yet appealed to the great name of Cyril. And there were saints again, Basil and others, appearing in suspected quarters, only slowly, and with searching of heart, to be recognized and admitted into loyal confidence. And all this anxiety, this confusion, this distress, let us remember, was not about some partial and limited detail of the faith. Nay; the storm was raging round the question of questions, round the cardinal and vital heart of the Creed, round the Person of the Lord Himself. It was a matter of life and death that was at stake.

That is the scene; those are the conditions out of which we won, to our everlasting peace, those calm, clear phrases of the Catholic Creeds. There they stand at last, perfect, strong, entire; so quiet and sure that we forget that the smell of fire has been upon them. We remember no more the anguish and trial out of which they were born. Those Creeds are the work of the Holy Ghost in the Church. So we rightly believe; but, so believing, we are apt to fancy that that must mean that they were done in a flash, in easy strength. God spoke, we suppose, and it was done. We have our fancy-picture of a Church that came together, with regular and calm despatch, at each difficulty that arose, and at once relieved all dispute and indecision by formally announcing the true Creed; and then we are staggered to find ourselves to-day deprived of this rapid and convenient mechanism, left to the strain and the pain of prolonged uncertainty, often stripped of authoritative guidance just when we seem most to need it, encompassed by obscurities, watching timorously the local interests, the temporary accidents, the worldly intrigues, which seem ever on the very point of doing some irretrievable hurt to the truth and the Church. But if we know facts, we escape this disturbing contrast ; for then we have learnt that the Creeds can indeed be the work of the Holy Spirit, and yet not be shown to be such by force of rapid ease, but rather by the victorious lordship perilously but perfectly exercised over the tumult and the chaos of earthly passion. The evidence for His presence is to be found in the contrast between the apparent disorder and terror of the outward scene and the steady and beautiful harmony of the result. To us it seems but a wild and confused babel of discordant noises, yet in its very midst, as we find, the Holy Spirit still worked. Still He held the threads and clues ; still He warded off the threatening disasters ; still He toiled and strove ; still He saved the remnant, He shielded the Holy Seed ; still He fashioned, in His holy fires, like a smith beats out and toughens iron, the strong words which should stand for ever ; still over the chaos of those loud waters He passed, and under Him the truth grew, came together, shaped itself, solid, firm, eternal ; and then the storm ceased, the wind died away, and there it stood—the fair and beautiful fabric, within which belief could find itself at peace ; there stood the Creeds, His own undoubted work, testifying to Him, the evidence of His care, of His teaching, of His tenacity, of His unfailing inspiration.

Now that we see the result, we do not doubt the Spirit's handling, any more than we doubt the evidence of the Creator's Mind and Will which is given us in the completed structure of the living bird. The subtlety and toil of the long process through the pressure of which it was formed cannot be allowed to obscure the positive and decisive clearness of the outcome. The proof of God's handling, of God's supremacy, is as undeniable in every line and point of that delicate mechanism of the swallow, as if He had struck it out with one blow of His hand, with one word of His Will. And as He works in nature, so, after the same methods and analogies, it has been in the framing of His supernatural kingdom. Through the very thick of human disorder He held on His predestined and unbroken way. The process to human eyes was dark, confused, slow, perilous; but lo! the fruit is peace. The Spirit, Whose track our eyes could not follow, has never failed His task. In spite of human wranglings, the truth has been secured; the Creed has been built, word by word, line after line; the victory is complete. Now we know the meaning, the issues, the gain of all those long, painful, patient hours, when men cried for the night to pass, and it seemed as if no dawn would ever break. Now we know. All is justified; all is safe. Verily "the Lord sitteth above the waterflood: and the Lord remaineth a King for ever."

Those others have laboured; we have entered into their labours. Others went forth to sow, weeping as they went; it is we who come with joy, bringing their sheaves with us. We feed on the strength of these calm Creeds, which they in labour, in agony, wrestled and fought and toiled to frame and to secure us. In the sweat of their brows we eat our bread, with glad hearts, to-day. But, then, we cannot suppose that we, who feast at ease on their winnings, will be spared our own portion of that chastening through which they passed to their victory. We enjoy the firm record of Christ's Person and dignity to which they, through much tribulation, found their way. That is made easy for us which to them was so hard. We can avoid the perils which pressed through them so sorely; we can see with clear eyes, we can speak with sure voice, where to them light was broken and utterance dangerous. But the discipline which they endured is as necessary as ever. If it was good for the Church to be shaken and tossed then, it is good for it still. If it was right then that men should have to wrestle and strive in order to attain the knowledge of the truth, in order to apprehend firmly what it is they believe, it must be right now for us. Nay; the more loyally we prize the Catholic Creeds, which were wrought out through such obscurity, and anxiety, and danger, the more we shall expect and be ready to find ourselves summoned to face new forms of danger, to endure fresh anxieties, to travel through the like obscurities. The right apprehension of Christ is an age-long discipline, a life-trial: it needs stings to prick us; it will be often an affair of buffets, and blows, and bruises. It can never be won without effort or without cost. And why, then, should we be so staggered at the perplexities which encompass the Church and imperil the faith? Those very Creeds which seem to stand in peace above our clamorous uncertainties and noisy disputes, are there to sanction and explain, by their own story, the confusions through which we are travelling, and the fears by which we are made miserable.

Let us remember their story and take courage to meet our own discipline. And two good comforts those Creeds supply to us, which were lacking to those who built them. For by possessing in our hands their firm phrases, we can never, even in our worst plight, fall into such desperate trouble as they endured who, in the fourth century, knew not where to turn for some voice which could assure them that they held the very faith of their fathers. For then it was the Person of our Lord Himself, His vital essence, which was the point in peril.

The Creeds then framed have secured to the Church for evermore the certain assurance of Who and What that Christ is Whom we worship. The questions that bewilder us now, *e.g.* about the nature of Christ's Church on earth, can never be quite so urgent or so awful as those which affect the nature of Christ Himself. We have those Creeds to hold by when all else looks troubled.

And then, secondly, those Creeds are a pledge to us that God does win results, win victories, throughout all our disorders and perplexities. Of old there was to the eye of man the like confusion as now; and yet we can now see clearly that God was still Master, at work then, sitting above the water-flood, shielding the holy seed, preserving the faith, watching over the Church, reaping good out of all the evil, building up the Catholic Creed in patience and in faithfulness; though His voice were not heard in the street, yet in mercy sparing to quench the smoking flax or to break the bruised reed, until He could at last bring out judgment unto victory. What He did then for them He will do now for us. As He won for Himself, out of that turmoil, the fruit of the Creeds, so some wonderful thing He is even now preparing and fashioning; some great issue, some fruit. Our confusions are serving His need; He is pruning, purging, purifying, chastening, educating, sanctifying His Church. And He will attain His end. He will bring out some judgment unto victory; He will reap a harvest; He will store His sheaves at last. We shall see and know, if we be but faithful now, what it was for which He bruised us, and we shall bless His Holy Name.

Let it suffice us that we have in us that same Holy Spirit, Who was sufficient for all their needs of old. He will guide us day by day along the road, though we know but little of what is happening, and see but little of what is being gained. Still in Him we can walk on and on, ever facing an obscurity, menacing and terrible, which will only yield, step by step, as we advance into its shadow. Yet yield it will, if only we advance in faith—yield it will; and ever again, as we face it anew, it will yet again yield and open. On will go the path, winding and shining; and ever there will be speaking the Voice behind us which says, day by day, according to our necessity, "This is the way; walk ye in it." Ever there will be the unspent Bread of Life, enough for the day; ever on the morrow we shall find that sacred Food again in the basket.

This is the walk of faith. Ah, how blessed! for it is the path by which the Father leads us. So they walked in its light, those of old whose words stand sure; so they walked in unflinching joy "troubled, but not distressed; perplexed, but not in despair; cast down, but not destroyed." So we, by God's grace, will walk, not asking to be spared what they endured.

> "They climbed the steep ascent of Heaven
> Through peril, toil, and pain;
> O God, to us may strength be given
> To follow in their train."

"*MADE UNDER THE LAW.*"

" When the fulness of the time was come, God sent forth His Son, made of a woman, made under the law."—GAL. iv. 4.

WE all know how largely the miraculous character of the Incarnation occupies our attention. The scientific advance in knowledge has brought a fierce pressure of criticism to bear upon this problem of the supernatural; the necessities of Christian apologetics have concentrated our interest upon that which is most under dispute. We cannot help this. We are bound, at all costs, to make good the full claims of our Lord Jesus Christ to His unique and absolute sovereignty; and such absolute sovereignty cannot be stated except in terms which will involve, of sheer inward necessity, miraculous results on the outward surface of that human life which He has filled with His own supremacy.

No, we cannot help it; we are bound to carry through the hot contention. But yet, if we were but at peace, if we were but left to follow out the natural course of reflection which the actual Incarnation suggests, unthwarted by side issues, it would be its naturalness rather than its supernaturalness which would most arrest and surprise us. That which is really startling in the Birth and Life of our Lord is, surely, not the extent of its miraculous display, but its strange and severe limitation; not the degree to which He exercised His Godhead, but the degree to which He emptied Himself of it. That is what bewilders and astounds us far more than any miracle. Men talk as if we Christians were brimming with a childish and reckless exuberance of supernaturalism. How distorted a misconception! Is not the wonder all the other way? Is it not amazing that a creed, which starts with such tremendous assertions about the Person of its Founder, should keep itself so well in hand, so rigidly under control, that its main force is spent in exhibiting the loyalty with which this only-begotten Son of God submitted to every ordinance of man and of nature, how He bent Himself down to the hard and narrow frontiers of His natural lot? For one man who is disturbed by the miracles we preach, there are twenty who are upset by the rigorous absence of miracle from our account of salvation. "Why this slow and painful dealing with sin and with sorrow?" they ask impatiently. "Why does not God act with greater freedom? Why does He not lay bare His holy arm? Why this roundabout method of redemption? Why this cruel insistence on His Son's suffering and death? Why give Him over to the hour of darkness? Why not take away the bitter cup? Why allow Him to be forsaken on the Cross? Why does He not uproot with a tempest the tyrannies of the oppressor? Why not break ye the strongholds? Why not rend the heavens and come down?" Ah, we know but too well the appeal, the passion, the misery of those questions! Those are the difficulties that bewilder and perplex hundreds of poor fretting, desolate hearts. And all these difficulties, what are they but a fierce protest against what we may call the unnatural naturalness of the Christian revelation—its strange, its startling repression of the miraculous, its abhorrence of all violent disturbance of the natural order? It is the cry for the twelve legions of angels; and the hotter our faith the more passionately we protest against the Lord's surrender of Himself to the Cross. "Nay! this be far from Thee, Lord! Why submit? Why pass under the yoke that all men wear? Why let things take their natural course? Why push nothing aside—thrust no cup from Thee—suffer what comes without resistance? Oh, impossible! This be far from Thee, Lord!" So spoke Peter of old, fervent and loving; but our Lord heard within his voice the whisper of the tempter, the adversary. For He, the Lord, had known already the terrible stress of that very temptation when, in His weary fast, full of the consciousness of the Spirit that had fallen upon Him, with all Power made His to exercise and to use, the whisper stole up into His ear: "If Thou be the Son of God, make these stones bread. If Thou be the Son of God, cast Thyself off the Temple-corner; His angels will bear Thee up." Yes, and now again the devil's whisper—"This be far from Thee," appealing to a truth—"If Thou be the Son of God;" it is the devil once more letting loose the old lie through the disguise of a friend: "Get thee behind me, Satan; thou savourest not the things that be of God, but those that be of man."

The Incarnation is the revelation of the binding force of natural law, to the necessities of which God Himself yields up His Son. It is the loud proclamation of the deference God pays to that Nature which is His own creation. Where, indeed, can we learn more emphatically than from the Cross of Christ, the validity, the sanctity of those natural conditions which God, of His own Will, obeyed, even to the Death of His Son, rather than break?

And to-day we keep the peculiar feast that

celebrates this Divine obedience. To-day our Blessed Lord is formally admitted within the normal and ordinary limitations of that human nature which He had assumed in the Virgin's womb. For He Who is come into the world to enlighten every man who is born, did not enter it in some miraculous freedom, to find the whole wide earth laid open, without bar or bolt, to His unhindered access. He bowed Himself to surrender His claim to direct and immediate possession of the entire humanity. He emptied Himself of all such privileged and easy liberty. He was spared nothing that was involved in taking the form of a slave. He had been "made of a woman," He had been "made under the law," born subject to all the accidents of place and time, born at a certain date and hour, drawn to the appointed and prophetic city, not by some supernatural intervention, but by the ordinary conditions of the imperial taxing, which had brought his Mother to the home of David, yet had so brought her that He had, in that city, no house in which to lay His head. And so born, He passes under the dread shadow of human history. He is encompassed round about with the thick intricacies of our black story. He takes His place in the long line of generations. He adds His Name to those who went before. He is inwoven into the meshes of a human pedigree. He becomes wholly ours, that we may become wholly His.

As we glance down that long list of our Lord's forefathers in S. Matthew or in S. Luke— which looks so stiff, and legal, and monotonous —how pathetic, how profound the significance becomes, as we remember what that list embodies! There, in those dry names, lies the record of the burden which the centuries had slowly built together for the Lord to carry. Through that line of names the story of man's life reached Him. It arrived to Him charged with all that those men had made it—their struggles, their hopes, their joys, their woes, their sins, their pains. Out of the nameless years which had come and gone, a certain sequence had preserved itself

O

through those remembered men, links in the long chain from Abraham and David. A tradition had handed itself down, a story had been prolonged, a memory had survived and grown, and accumulated details, and gathered in continuous experiences. Passions, aspirations, miseries, losses—all had stored their results within this unbroken and enduring movement. Such strange exaltations, such untoward reverses, such patient persistence, such stubborn obscurity, had all gone to the fashioning of that family of David! Into it had passed much that was worthiest and much that was worst of human character and incident. Ruth, and David, and Zerubbabel, pastoral loyalty, royal glories, heroic deliverances—yes, but also, as S. Matthew seems to suggest with frequent emphasis, Tamar, with her terrible scandal; Rahab, harlot of Jericho; and Bathsheba, the wife of David's sin. And all this inheritance, just as it stood, at the particular moment when Cæsar first prepared to lay the bitterest mark of servitude upon the race which once had tasted the free royalty of David, just when one of the last and humblest sons of that great king had Himself to acknowledge the servitude by enrolling Himself for a foreign tax, enrolling Himself for the tax of the conqueror, at the very city which enshrined His last ancestral glories—all this, without turning one jot or tittle of it aside, without shrinking, without refusal, our Lord assumed for His own on the day when He was carried to the Temple as the Child of Mary.

Nor was it only the burden of His parentage which He had to assume. He undertook also all the accumulated responsibilities which belonged to Him as the registered heir of Joseph, as a Son of the Covenant, as a Jew, circumcised the eighth day under the Name of *Jesus*. By that act He took His place in the historic order of Israel's development. That Circumcision brought down upon Him the whole weight of the Law, the entire and immense burden of Scripture, the long and painful discipline of Prophet and Redeemer.

He passed under the Law. He became a Son

of the covenant, a Jew of Jews, being already a child of Abraham. Two thousand years of continuous and recorded history laid hands upon Him by that act—two thousand years since first God had sealed His promise to man under the pledge of Circumcision. All that history stands good still. Christ accepts it; God respects it. None of it shall be destroyed or set aside. The Law is bound to be fulfilled, to be worked out; yea, to the very end. Only by complete and fearless submission to its claims can its dire necessities ever be loosed.

And not only under the Law; but He passed also under the Scripture. Here was the power of prophecy that went before Him. It accomplished its completed mission by lodging itself on Him, Who now, first at the hands of aged Simeon in the Temple, and yet again under the penitential ministry of the Baptist by Jordan, bent His neck of His own will, to the yoke, and set Himself to the hard task of fulfilling all our righteousness. The Jewish Scriptures, the spiritual record of

God's own prophetic handling of those chosen souls, who before the light shone should bear witness to its shining—those Scriptures now closed round that little Child with authoritative embrace, as Simeon lifted the Messiah long desired in his arms before God on the holy hill of Zion. What those books recorded He must now fulfil. The experiences there noted and stored had authority over Him. They gave Him His direction; they marked down the path He must tread. He is made responsible for all that faithful souls, in the weary years behind Him, had, under the discipline of the Spirit, been led to suffer, feel, utter, hope, declare. He accepts the limitations set upon Him by their intuitions. He consents to travel by the road that they have cast up, passing from stone to stone there where they of old, in days of darkness and agony, laid them in the wilderness. All their voices, all their cries, their beseechings, their protests, He will re-utter, He will reiterate. As they had been, so would He be. If they had been pierced in the house of their friends, even so would He be pierced. If they had gall and vinegar given them when their lips were parched with burning pain, so, too, shall He be not ashamed to taste of their cup. If but one of them had been sold for the contemptible price of a slave, that, too, should be His portion. If they had deemed themselves forsaken of God in the hour of their worst distress, He, too, would know what that horror of great darkness might mean. Whatever they had known—shame, spitting, scorn, infamy, cruelty, death—all should be passed on from them to Him; on His shoulders those stripes of theirs should fall, until all should have in Him an end, until all should in Him be fulfilled. So He was to walk in strict and careful submission to the lines set down for Him by this prepared past. Enough for Him that a sorrow should be recorded in those ancient books; He will Himself endure its repetition out of loyalty to those of old who felt the bitterness of its bruising. No legions of angels shall rush in to ward off from Him disaster, for that would be to fail His God-given task. "How, then, would the Scriptures be fulfilled?" So He walks, step by step, in the track of prophecy. Betrayal by Judas, desertion by those dearest, death by the hands of His own chosen people—all of this is accepted and justified out of faithful obedience to bygone experiences, to the limits set Him under His constant phrases: " It must needs be that the Scripture be fulfilled ;" " Ought not Christ to have suffered these things?" "The Son of Man goeth as it was determined ;" " I say unto you that that which is written must yet be accomplished ;" "These things were done that the Scripture might be fulfilled ;" " This all was done that it might be fulfilled which was spoken by the Prophet." And all this became His, to achieve by formal ratification, on the day when He was brought into the Jewish covenant, and was sealed to its conditions and necessities— the day when He was taken up by His parents on the eighth day to be circumcised, and received the Name of Jesus.

So "God sent His Son, made of a woman, made under the law." In how sharp a contrast this Divine method of reform, of revolution, stands to the declaration of the greatest of the idealists in the days before the Christ. Plato, as he sorrowfully reviewed the actual Athens with which he found himself encircled, pronounced, in his prophetic work on human society, that its true reformer and saviour would be known by this mark—that he would demand for himself a clean canvas before he consented to begin. He could do nothing unless he were allowed to remove from out of the influence and tradition of their home a whole generation of children; so alone could he obtain the clean canvas he needed. Ah, yes; if only the weary burden of our inherited complication could be thus freely cast off! If only we could lay hands, in the violence of love, on the little children, and sweep them off into some new Garden of Eden! If only we could run a sharp dividing knife between us and the rueful past! Surely there is a deep and touching pathos in that demand, which stirs us into tender admiration of the noble-hearted genius who made it. But its pathos must not disguise from us that it is a confession of failure, of impotence, of despair. The reformer who asks first for a clean canvas to begin upon, is a reformer who refuses to grapple with his task, refuses to face his facts. He condemns himself by making the demand; for what is asked of him is that he should help us to better the life that now is, the situation in which he and we find ourselves. We do not need him to tell us how well he could construct another form of life under changed conditions. No; it is the very note of all the old failure to redeem the world by philosophy which is struck in the sad Platonic phrase, "Give me but the children—give me a clean canvas!"

"The clean canvas!" Ah, how well we ourselves know the temptation of that demand—we who are so pitifully overloaded with the weight of ancient wrongs; we who are pursued and harried by the avenging Furies for our past social misdeeds. We are netted in such thick meshes. This poverty that appals us, how far back does its original spring lie; how deep dug its roots, its causes! Alas! back and back we track them, and our hearts die within us, and we grow faint, and weary, and puzzled, and bewildered. Can we ever secure firm ground? Can we ever undo the cruel knots and hateful tangles? The closer we study the economical conditions of wealth, the darker and vaster grows the desperate problem. And if there be those among us who cannot tolerate a depression, a degradation, that seems bound to increase in spite of our best efforts; if there be those who, under the pressure of the sights they see and the cries they hear, become impatient and lose control, and seek impatiently some outlet of escape, and repudiate the inheritance that has come down to them, and demand that some decisive act should sever us from the weary past; if there be those who demand the clean canvas and the new social start;—surely we shall enter into the pathos of their cry; surely we shall understand the sway of their temptation, we shall be very gentle with their righteous impatience, even though we know that their demand is a confession of their failure, or a proof of their helplessness, or an echo from their despair; even though we remember how different was the courage of our own Master, Who asked for no violent or miraculous interference with those limitations by which the past conditioned the advance, asked for no legions of angels to force for Him an open highway. No; the past shall indeed be put away, and the limitations shall indeed be mastered and overpowered; but this can only be done by One Who has faith enough in the power of God to take first upon His own shoulders all the sorrow and the sin which that past has transmitted—faith enough in the victorious Spirit to bend His head in submission to all the limitations which the long ages had built and bonded—faith enough to bury Himself within the very heart of the actual situation as it stood, and from thence, from within, as the leaven hidden within the lump, to work in patience, in penitence, in invincible loyalty, in unwearied hope, until the corrupted mass itself becomes transformed, renewed, transfigured.

"Give me a clean canvas." We hear the same beseeching voice go up again and again from those who are wearied with the battle of the creeds, and sick to death of the quarrels of Christians. Here again history has passed down to us a long, wearisome, woeful tale. In England, above all, where the story of the Church is so strangely and deeply interwoven with the story of the people and the throne, the Catholic faith of Christ arrives at our late generation, bearing along with it the complications, the incumbrances, the *débris*, the ruins, of all that has gone to the confused making of a nation's existence. It comes to us marred, and maimed, and scarred, and bruised. And, oh, how we sigh for the simplicity of some early day, when to believe was at least to know what one believed; when to belong to the Church was to enter a brotherhood of purity, a home of peace! And no wonder that men get impatient, and would sweep out of sight all this huge obstacle which time and the sad years have built between them and the Master Whom they would love. They would ignore all that has happened, all that has come between. They would go back behind it all, and recover the lost cue—go back behind this confused, distracted, Anglican story to seek some clear papal authority, some universal Roman voice; or, if that be not enough, go back yet again behind the Roman historical entanglements to find some unbewildered Church of the Fathers into whose happy garden no serpent of schism had ever crept; or, if that search prove vain, go back behind the stormy story of the dogmatic creeds to look for some clear and open Bible, which all can lightly read and understand, without confusion and without risk; or, if still the questions thicken, imagine that they yet may go back behind the terrible metaphysics of the Pauline Epistles, to the secure simplicity of the four Gospels; or, if trouble still haunt them, then go back behind the miracles of the Gospels, and the agitating discussion of their authorship, and the critical analysis of their perplexing formation, to dig for some Christianity which was Christ's own before ever it passed away from Him to become distorted in the minds of His first followers—back to explore some far, happy, simple, unencumbered Christianity which was in our Lord's Mind, but yet never succeeded in making itself known to any one until it was sifted out at last, eighteen hundred years after, by some ardent and earnest seeker, from the records which had themselves misunderstood and corrupted it. So pathetic, so hopeless, that familiar search after a flying phantom! We will not be angry at a task which condemns itself to inevitable failure—condemns itself by seeking to escape from the actual conditions of the problem which it sets itself to unravel; not angry, rather patient and compassionate. While yet we brace ourselves to recall how we stand pledged by our Lord's Circumcision, pledged by His voluntary submission to the conditions of His Birth and Parentage, pledged by this, to be ourselves loyal to the actual historical literature, loyal to the facts, loyal to the known and recorded story through which the faith of Christ has historically passed, loyal to the continuous tradition in the form in which it has reached us. We will bide loyal to the ship of Christ's Church, though storms have battered it, and the waves have shaken it, and the winds have roared against it, and the salt seas, many and bitter, have washed through it and over it. We will be loyal—loyal to the date at which we have been born into Christ's Body; loyal to the long years through which our fathers, amid distress and disaster, have yet striven to hand down to us the truth that they received; loyal to our high Christian pedigree, that knits us up to king, and saint, and martyr of old heroic days; yes, loyal to it, even though there be woven into its tale scandals as terrible as Tamar's, memories as unhappy as those of Bathsheba and Rahab.

"The clean canvas!" How many of us in our

hearts are uttering that vain desire for themselves: "Give me, O God, a clean canvas; then I could reform. I cannot go on in this weary battle, so mixed and so broken, against my sins! But if only I could be as if nothing had been; if only I were given 'a clean canvas;' if only the old horrid memories did not haunt me still, long after I have repudiated the deeds that bred them; if only I were not tangled in the issue of rejected lusts and repented lies; if only the dreary weight of past blunders were lifted off; if only I could go straight on along the better path, which I do indeed desire, and not lapse, and stumble, and fall again and yet again; if only other people would help me more, and my home were not such as it is, and my life were not so oppressed by things for which I am not responsible; if only the canvas were clean!" Yes, if only facts were not facts; if only the past were not the past! Poor, pitiful cry of the wounded soul, so pathetic and so vain! God indeed offers a new beginning; Christ indeed makes all things new; but it is you, yourself, as you are, which He asks for. It is this that He would redeem and recover—you, the very self in you, which is now sick, and wounded, and loaded, and broken. This is what He wants; not some imaginary self dropped out of the skies, without a past, without a story. You are to bring yourself, with all your actual load of evil memories, with all your sins, confessed, acknowledged, unexcused—yourself, damaged, fainthearted, worn, diseased. He accepts you, He rejects nothing, if only you be cast at His feet. Come, bring Him all; confess all; resign yourself to all that the bad years have now made inevitable. God cannot spare you the slow and painful work of remedy, but He can and will give you His own force to endure it. Here is the one miracle, the only miracle you need. Deep within all He will lodge His Spirit; back behind all He will implant Himself. There is your security; there is your new start. In Christ, Who is made yours, old things are become dead; you are made new. Sure of that, you will not be afraid, what-

P

ever the year brings you. Sore and heavy, the slow hours will often creep along; burdensome and dreary the load you may have yet to carry far; but be of good heart, step out with courage, for, within, He will not fail you, Who, circumcised the eighth day, asked for Himself no legion of angels, nor even to relieve Himself, would turn stones into bread.

THE DIVINE SANCTION TO NATURAL LAW.

"Therefore, O thou son of man, speak unto the house of Israel; Thus ye speak, saying, If our transgressions and our sins be upon us, and we pine away in them, how should we then live? Say unto them, As I live, saith the Lord God, I have no pleasure in the death of the wicked; but that the wicked turn from his way and live: turn ye, turn ye from your evil ways; for why will ye die, O house of Israel?"—EZEK. xxxiii. 10, 11.

THE more we reflect, the more wonderful it seems that we should ever have supposed that the Christian creed had failed to take sufficient account of the authority of law and nature; so laborious, so painstaking, so elaborate, so profound, is its recognition of the obligations imposed upon it by natural conditions, to which it is bound, at all hazards, to conform.

Yet what a Divine restraint did not conformity imply!

The world before Christ was surely clamouring aloud for some heroic and miraculous intervention. Everything in it cried out for some violent handling, for some breach in its natural continuity, so dismal was the outlook, so tangled the web, so deep-rooted the wrong, so irredeemable the blunders, so hateful the disorder, so base the fall, so foul the corruption, so hideous the sin, so cruel the hurt. Who with a heart to feel, with a spirit to love, could tolerate any longer that accumulating agony? Even we, with our full knowledge, our secure possession, of the secret revealed through the tender compassion of the Divine Sufferer crucified for us, can hardly keep our souls patient under the stress of wickedness and misery, as they lay hands at large upon the weltering masses of our fellows, or, perhaps worse, as they creep, with sure and stealthy step, to fasten their fierce claws into life after life of those whom we know, and watch, and love, at our side, in our home, amid our circle. One after another we see them pass under the shadow; the horrid thing has them, holds them—a sin, a loss, something disastrous closes in upon them; their bright hopefulness is smitten; the dank, wet fog settles down upon them. One by one they suddenly look at us with scared eyes of alarm. "The curse is on us," they cry; "it is come even unto us. We heard of it before by the hearing of the ear; now we see it. Lo! we are stricken by the old grievous wound; our joy is wrecked; here on earth is no peace—only sorrow, only sighing, only tears. Woe is it! for we were so young, so full of hope, so innocent once, so merry-hearted. We thought that all was well. And now we too join the great army of the mourners; we take our places amid the multitudes of those who have loved and lost— have loved, and have ruined and sinned away their love." So the bitter story drags on its weary, weary length, ever renewing its melancholy repetitions; and even we become impatient, we who have the consolation. What, then, of those who had, before Christ, become sensitive as we, whose culture was wide as ours, whose hopes were as large, whose nerves were as high-strung, whose disappointment was as intense—of those in that vast Roman world who sickened with our sickness, and felt the weight of a world-wide disaster, and yet were without any care, interpretation, promise? No wonder if their faith died away in a wail of desperate confession: " There is no God—no God at all! How, if there be, can He endure that such sorrow and suffering should exist, and He make no sign? There is no God, then, since the curse bides on, unbroken, undispelled. There is no Hand that guides, controls, governs; there is no Heart beholds, pities, delivers. Nay; it is no longer the mere petulance of the fool that says, 'There is no God.' It is the deliberate and calm judgment of the wise, the thoughtful, the cultivated, the sober. It is this which pronounces, through quiet lips, the despairing decision, 'There can be no God;' or, 'If there be a God, He cares not at all for us miserable men. He sits on some far throne in idle security, in careless ease, and up into His ears our pitiful cry only enters "as a tale of little meaning," as some ancient burden of a woeful song which we hear in a faint dream. So far is God, so careless, so unhelping—if there be a God at all in that silent, awful heaven.'"

So the great pagan world gave voice to man's despair; and over against that bitter confession there rose but one strong and historic cry of protest—the voice of the one people who never lost their ancient trust, never dropped the thread, never fainted altogether, nor grew quite weary. Battered and bruised though they were by a fate as dark and violent as any to which the faiths of others succumbed; invaded, shattered, vanquished by trampling armies — Assyrian, and Grecian, and Roman—still they held on with heroic tenacity; still they faced all with their invincible profession, "There is a God. Though He hide Himself, though He seem to forsake and forget, yet doubtless He is still our Father; He is still strong, almighty, true. He inhabiteth eternity, high and holy. There is a God; at all costs we believe that. Nothing can shake us out of that faith; nothing can tear it out of our souls. We remember the days of old; we go back and rehearse the old proofs and pledges. There is a God, one God, Who made, Who rules, Who must prevail. And because there certainly is a God, therefore we know that He will one day lay bare His holy arm; He will sweep out of sight all our misery and oppression; He will come, and with a recompense. There will be a day; though it tarry long we are sure of it. After two days He will return and restore; on the third day He will revive us. We look for that Messianic day. We wait on and on for Him. How long, how long! Yet we will be found waiting. Then all shall vanish like an evil dream in the clear morning; our Redeemer shall stand upon Mount Zion. From Bozrah, from Edom, we shall see Him, vengeance in His hand. 'They shall not hurt or destroy in all My holy mountain.'"

So either argued—the Roman, and the Jew: "The curse remains unabolished, the misery bides unhealed, therefore there is no God." "There is a God; therefore the curse, the misery, will all be swept away when He comes."

And what happened? To the Greek, foolishness; to the Jew, a stumbling-block. God came; God entered. The Jew was right; his stubborn confidence was justified, his prophecy was verified. God is; God rules; God cares; God loves; God is sure to come and save. The Jew alone of all nations stood approved. Yes, God enters the earth to deliver; but, nevertheless, what a shock, what a blow, awaits the poor, hoping, clinging, invincible heart of the Jew! God enters, yet not to sweep the curse out of sight, but to pass under it Himself, "to become the curse." He comes, not to abolish suffering, but to endure it; not to remove the pain, but to share it; not to break the yoke of the oppressor, but to put His own neck under the yoke.

Look over the wide face of earth now that Christ has been born in Bethlehem, look over that Roman Empire as the eye of man would see it; hardly a quiver could be traced of change on the outer surface—no disturbance, no disruption, no suspension. Those that suffer, suffer still; those that die, die still; the tyrannies, the miseries, all keep their clutch. God, in the Person of the Son, has slid Himself within them, beneath them, almost without a sign, or sound, or motion, except to the very few who have faith to discover, to follow Him.

What does it mean ? It means that God, even in the miraculous act by which He repels and arrests our curse, still respects nature, respects law. This weary weight of woe that loads and crushes our souls down into the dust of death is no accident, no external blot, that can be lightly or violently removed. It is the due and certified effect of a wrong past. As a result—a lawful, and necessary, and natural result of certain causes—it is perfectly justifiable. God Himself authorizes its necessity ; God Himself acknowledges its right to be what it is ; God Himself puts His seal upon it, by His own submission to its terrible authority. As a sorrow consequent on broken covenant, and neglected law, and defiled purity, it is to be recognized and justified. God enters the earth to call our attention to this, to justify us in submitting to and enduring it. "The soul that sinneth, it must die." God may indeed go beyond that law, but suspend it, ignore it, He cannot; for it is Himself Who creates the law. We speak often as if the fact that God made a law is a reason why He should be able to change or reverse it at will. But that is only true of an external and legal enactment; it is not true, in the deepest sense of law, as the principle of existence. In this sense, the fact that God is the Author of the law is the reason, not why He is able to change or reverse it, but why He cannot do so. He must respect, He must honour, His own Will in so creating things in the way He did. That Will was no arbitrary act which created the world, as a child does a toy, or even as an artisan puts together a machine, or an artist designs a building or a picture. The child may abandon its toy, the artisan may vary his machine, the artist may re-create his handiwork; but God is no artificer, no artist, in His character as a Creator. These are but thin and inadequate symbols of what we mean by creation. Creation is a far more intimate act, in which the author does not merely manufacture into definite shape and order some given material, as the potter his clay, to be broken up again and varied as he will. That metaphor only expresses certain partial and limited aspects of God's power. Creation is the act of will by which the material itself, together with all its possibilities and conditions, comes into existence; and creation, whatever else it may involve, however hard, however impossible, for us to picture or to explain, must at least be an exertion of energy which involves and implicates the reason, the will, the love of God Himself. It implicates His reason, which expresses itself in the processes by which the created life acquires and assumes its organic structure; it involves His will, which comes out from Him to appear under the forms of motion and force, to make and build the fabric of life; it implicates His love, which goes out from Him to fill the life with growth, and aspiration, and desire, and to set it all in upward movement towards an ideal and sufficient end.

Divine love, Divine will, Divine reason—all these have gone to the effort of creation; all have passed out into the living thing, to construct, sustain, develop it. No analogy, therefore, drawn from the workshop of the artisan or the artist will give more than a mere shadow, a faint symbol, of the closeness of the intimacy which holds between God and His creation. And above all, in the case of man. Here there is but one metaphor God sanctions as interpreting His full, inward relationship. It is that of father and child. Man is made "in His image"—is as His child. Man, the whole man, mankind, the race of man as an integral mass—this is His child. Not merely some selected holy spirits drawn out of it into closer communications with Himself. No! Man, as a single created thing, is stamped with the image of the Divine Sonship of the Word, is summed up in the incarnate Sonship of Jesus Christ. Who can measure or track the inwoven intricacies of this intimate relationship? Here, indeed, is no toy that can be broken up; no mere machine that can be taken to pieces and remade; no picture, to be wiped out and painted again. Here is no stranger, who can be rejected if unworthy and hopeless; no foe, who can be trodden underfoot for his guilty aggression. No; all these images fail us. Here is a child, the issue of a Divine desire, the embodiment of an inward hope, of a passionate act of love. What can break this tie? How will God ever fail to be loyal to His fatherhood? True, the child is faithless, defiled, wicked, miserable; and true, terribly true, that, being wicked, it is necessarily doomed, by sheer consequence of the Divine reason in which it was created, to sickness, wretchedness, pain, death. "The soul that sinneth, it must die." It dies by sinning. God has so made it that the wages of its sin are its death. That terrible law permits of no breach. It may be met, counteracted, forestalled, arrested; its accumulated force, gathered through the increasing guilt of the crowded past, may be diverted, transmuted, absorbed, translated; but the thing that can never be is that it should be denied, abolished, suspended, prohibited. The child of God has deeply sinned, and, as deeply sinning, it must be subject to the inevitable law, which God cannot repudiate without repudiating the reason, the will, the love, with which He created His child. "It must die."

And yet it is His child; He is still its Father. Surely He has no pleasure in the death of the wicked; His Fatherhood still pleads against the fateful doom. Any violent, rigorous, sweeping act of judgment, such as men prayed for, such as the holier and purer men looked for under the agony of their darkness, such as those who were most anxious for God's honour, so long obscured, most eagerly and loudly desired—an act that would scatter the wicked as a whirlwind, or would chase them as the stubble before the wind—any such act would seal the destiny of those, God's children, who would necessarily perish in the death of sin. And God, the great Father, cannot be content with rescuing out of trouble and suffering the few who were holy, the few whose faith could be counted to them for righteousness, if it was at the cost of losing any of those wicked ones who might yet be won, who, wicked though they were, were yet so intimately His own.

Ah! are we not in this still discovering ourselves to be caught in the snare which trapped the Gnostics of the first centuries? The Gnostic, full of his Platonic dualism, thought always of a holy seed imprisoned within a mass of carnal wickedness, from out of which God was concerned in delivering it. The redemption is only a scheme by which God reaches down out of heaven a hand to touch, and raise, and release those special souls that were His. By it they passed up out of their lower and fleshly degradation into the high purity of spiritual existence; the rest, who were carnal in themselves, were left to their appropriate sphere. How tempting the pleasant creed! Yet the early Church knew the pressure of holy repulsion to such a belief; she saw that it was but a caricature of her own belief. Christ came down, she knew well, not to liberate the elect from an unworthy and hateful imprisonment among the wicked, but to redeem the wicked, the sinners, whom He still loved. "While we were yet sinners, Christ died for the ungodly." That was her starting-point. The whole human race was on a level, so far as wickedness went. There was no distinction of merit, no distinction of status, which could permit of a line being drawn between the spiritual and the carnal seed. Not one, no, not one could say, "I am not as those others, I am not as those publicans. Rescue me, my God, from a position so degrading to me, so far below my worth, from my imprisonment within a vile companionship." Here was the very prayer which S. Paul so triumphantly convicted, which our Lord so profoundly loathed. Perish the terrible Pharisaic pride! If S. Peter himself be trapped into anything approaching a recognition of such a distinction, let S. Paul, at all risk, withstand him to the face. It is as sinners, as one with the wicked, that we are all saved in Christ's blood, elect and all, or we are not saved at all; and therefore we and those others who lie yet in their wickedness are one thing, one mass, one humanity, one issue of God's Fatherhood, one object of His love. Christ died for all, for the entire sum of the human race, if He died for any. This is the very root of our faith.

Yes, but let us face all the consequences. We cannot, if this be the heart of our faith, clamour because God tarries long, because the day of the Lord lingers yet; cannot complain because the godly are left to suffer, undelivered, unavenged; cannot complain because sorrow, and sighing, and tears are not all swept away from those blessed and dear ones who believe in Christ. To rescue the faithful, to bring in the day of the redeemed, to wipe off the tears from their eyes, is to hasten the judgment, is to hurry up the final severance of good and evil. It must mean this; and though the spirit of the faithful must long for this deliverance, must pray its prayer, "Come, Lord Jesus," yet always this most right desire will be crossed by the thought of Epiphany, of the dark thousands who still repel the light, of those who perversely lie still in the darkness of evil. For that day cannot come without fixing the fate of those who yet choose sin. It must necessarily slay the wicked; and they are God's children; they have been bought for Him again by Christ's blood. Christ died for them; out over them goes the mighty intercession of our great High Priest; out over them His arms are spread wide; up before God for them ascend His pleadings. Can nothing be done? Is there not yet a hope that they may turn from their ways and live? "O turn ye, turn ye, ye house of Israel! Have I any pleasure in the death of the wicked?" saith the Lord.

Do we understand, then, why God should enter the world, and yet leave it to follow on its course, leave it to work out its career, without some summary and violent precipitation of the crisis? The Gnostic, looking only to the interests of the elect, has no regard for, no interest in, the natural man, with his unhappy and blundering and blotted history; he only desires to escape his evil company. But God, in Christ, honours His own natural creation; honours human nature; honours, respects, mourns over, loves His wandering, disgraced, contemptible prodigal out there, naked and hungry, among the swine. He does not forget, even where a father might forget, nor forsake, even where a mother might forsake. No, He will defer judgment; He will delay the crisis; He will set Himself to forestall the doom that must work itself out as the issue of sin. He will endure our sins, rather than lose a soul that can be saved. He sets Himself to win the entire body back again, vile and miserable as it is.

For God willed that none should perish; He willed that all should be summed up in Christ. He put out in Christ enough force to rescue, heal, cleanse, renew, glorify the entire body of mankind. Even if, at the last, there will be found a residue of stubborn defiance in the human will, which can hold out against the fullest effort of Divine pardon, yet that will be only through wilful refusal to suffer the whole will of God to make itself good; still it will remain true that the intention, purpose, hope of God is that in Christ every soul should be brought to repentance. And, if so, we must not sink the scale because the hope seems to us so distant and so broken. We must measure the Father's actions according to the width and breadth of His perfect scheme.

Let us ask ourselves, Are we faithful to this measure, when we get impatient with God's delays, when we fret at His long-suffering? Have we well in view His splendid and wonderful aim? Do we remember that His Father's heart is turned towards all those who are our trial and affliction; towards all those with whom we are so angry; towards the whole dead weight of blind indifference, so aggravating, so base; towards those who triumph in their wickedness and override His judgments? He is still seeking for them, He is still desiring their salvation; still the memory of that awful and irrevocable law haunts Him: "The soul that sinneth, it must die." These souls that sin, they must die if they cannot yet be won to repentance; they must die if God hurry on the last catastrophe. The judgment of God is the ultimate and victorious assertion of law ; and by law, by necessity, these souls are doomed. Only His Christ intervenes between them and the end. If only they might yet find their way to Him ! He yearns in pity : " Why, why will ye die ? " Oh, surely we too would lift up our hearts and join our prayers to those of the Great Intercessor. Not some rash prayer, " How long, how long ? " but rather, " Yet a little longer withhold Thy hand, O God ! It matters not that the world treads down Thy Church ; that the wild boars out of the wood devour Thy vineyard ; that we are sad, and sick, and miserable, and cowed, and beaten, and hurt. We can suffer ; we can wait. But those others ! 'O Father, forgive them ; they know not what they do.' "

If we were only free from the wretched narrowness of Gnosticism, from thinking that everything is for the sake of the elect, of the believers, we should not be so distressed that the faithful are allowed to abide in the thick of such trouble and pain. The elect exist for the sake of the wicked world; they are God's instruments for reaching, touching, converting the world. As their Master lived and died on behalf of a godless world, even so are they in the world. Is their task complete? Is their use over? To call upon God to finish with the world, to bring in the end, to free His saints, is to confess that no more of the world can ever be won to God; that the frontier of Christ's redemptive efficacy has been touched; that the mastery of the Cross has no more disclosures to make of its prevailing power; that we have come to the limit of Christ's Epiphany; that our task of lighting the world is of no more avail. What a pitiful confession! What a coward cry! What a faithless faith!

Let us be brave enough to believe that the world may yet be won, that Christ has many a victory before Him. This hope will buoy us up; for it will explain to us why God keeps in the far background, why He hideth Himself, why He suffers such long years to go wearily past with their hideous story. We shall recognize the dauntless and invincible mercy of God that spares, and lingers, and hopes on ; and so we shall not despair of God, even though we have to see what now we see, the terrible strength of the world's power—even though we have to listen on to the lies by which a corrupt society justifies its corruption, to the hollow conventionalisms by which public opinion caresses itself into indolence, to the cries of innocent children, on whom the lusts of their fathers break out in plagues. We shall not despair of Christ, even though we have to watch whole herds of people, comfortable and flourishing, who have never done anything but harm to the social order which sustains them, who have never for one moment paused from their wicked race after pleasure to take the measure of their responsibilities, and to ask what their idleness or their luxury are doing to the poor brothers and sisters who starve at their doors! No; when the passion of anger rises in our blood we will beat it back. Austere as we must be against the cruelty of the sins, we will yet remember always —Christ died for these souls; Christ still pleads with these sinning souls. Unless they will at last hear Him, they will die!

And if at some darker hours our hearts sink, and we wonder whether anything is being achieved, whether our hope can be real, whether it can be worth while to wait on and trust, then, beloved, let us remind ourselves that we have no gauge by which to measure the gains and the losses. We are not in a position to estimate God's winnings, for we know not yet what we all shall be hereafter; we know not what God has in view, in store. His ultimate aim is hidden far, far beyond the veil of death. And in view of that hereafter He may well be gaining more than we think out of this dark and chaotic probation on earth. For God gains if only He can save a soul from that deliberate and defiant recoil from holiness which makes the case desperate; He gains if only He can secure in a soul that its deepest wish, its core of will below all its wretched, woe-begone falls and defilements, have something in it of belief in goodness, of appeal to God—retain some inner motion at its root, which issues out of life's trials with an upward and not a downward tendency. If only He can win this, then there are at least some possibilities hereafter; there is something secured which the discipline and the purging of spiritual penitence can develop, cherish, and quicken. That soul will not have fallen outside the working of Christ's atonement. It may be saved, though as by fire, though after many stripes.

And who can say what possibilities of this kind are not being kept open by the presence, amid the throngs of a wicked world, of some rare saints of God—some rare and holy souls, who all their days may have felt themselves lost, broken, depressed, forlorn, girdled in by seething sins of men, which they could not restrain, or rebuke, or put to shame? So it had seemed to them. All their life had been a desperate defeat, and they passed out in neglected deaths, and the world rolled on its triumphant way more audaciously than ever. So it seemed to their sad eyes as they sighed for the far hidden Jerusalem. And yet, ever as they moved about, the hearts even of those who laughed them down and went on in their old, bad sins—even the hearts of these had all the time felt a strange touch of inner attraction, a strange quiver of spiritual recognition. Even as they rejected their message and scorned and drove them under, yet this one and that had said quietly, far down in their buried selves, " Those are good men ; they are better than I. I would I were as they ! " So they whispered, and that dim recognition may have saved them for Christ. The Sonship of God, choked and baffled within them, woke and stirred ; though it may not have had strength to reach the surface of life, to change habits, to reverse currents, it was there ; it abode ; it did not pass ; it preserved itself as the salt of their secret character ; and on their dying beds, with nothing but a life of selfish, indolent, heedless, useless, insolent sin to look back upon, they still will have never lost the conviction that then came home to them. Still they will say, " I never knew any one half so good as that saint whom I once mocked at. He made me feel how bad I am ; his memory has made confession and repentance possible to me. I should like to have lived as he; would that my last end could have been as his!" So he dies, and, so dying, there is one more soul just snatched out of the jaws of the lion, just saved for Christ to purge—a contemptible, disgraced, cowardly, ugly, foul soul, if you like, but yet not hating holiness, not preferring sin, and therefore rescued from the pit, from the unutterable doom; and over it, therefore, some faint song may go out of the angels that watch in heaven, and God may be glad to pronounce that at least it was good for that soul that it had been born. Ah! who can say what is going on about us? How startling now and again to us the sudden revelation of some deep-lying heart of grace, within those whom we deemed the worst and most hopeless! Behind walls of deformity that drunkenness and lust and cruelty have built and soldered, some wonderful movement, secret, miraculous, discovers itself, of profound, pathetic penitence, of passionate chivalry, that puts us all to shame. Yes, though the sinners be very many and the saints very few, it may be that their scattered presence saves the bad man from sinking—keeps possibilities open. The salt of the faithful may be doing far more than we can ever guess in keeping open channels, narrow and pinched it may be, but at least clean, by which the mercy of God can enter in and retain its hold upon a fallen world, which may yet be rescued.

So we will plod on to the end; we will not ask to count God's gains. Hereafter, oh, how blessed the joy, if, indeed, by God's grace, it be given to any of us, to learn all the futility of our childish impatience, as we are shown by the Spirit the real harvest that Christ was ever reaping, off fields that once looked to us so desolate and barren. This may be ours hereafter, if we be not all unfaithful to the blood of sprinkling; and for the present we will desire not to be taken out of the world, but to be kept from its evil. For the present let it be enough that the Lord direct our hearts unto the patient waiting for Christ.

"THE WORD WAS MADE FLESH."

"And the Word was made flesh, and dwelt among us, and we beheld His glory, the glory as of the only-begotten of the Father."
—S. JOHN i. 14.

WE may often find ourselves bewildered by the double language with which the Christian faith treats this earthly human life. On the one hand, at Christmastide, and all through Epiphany, we are full of happy speech, that tells of peace and goodwill to all mankind; tells of wise men from afar, who bring to the new-born King the gifts and treasures of earth, to find in Him their true benediction; tells of waiting water that receives into itself, at a glad marriage feast, the red, rich flush of approving grace. Christ is come "to be the Light of the world, the Light of every man." He comes as the illumination which solves all riddles, and interprets all parables, and fulfils all anticipations, and opens all secrets, and closes all stories, and realizes all efforts, and consummates all preparatory types. He holds the royal key of David, and at His entry all doors unlock, and all things fall into their place and order. Christ is the Light and Crown and Sum of human life, and, as such, we are not surprised to find that, through faith in Him, society receives a new sanction, a fuller development. The typical human institution of marriage, round which all social existence turns, is transfigured by Christ's appearance. He finds in it the symbol and law of His own relation to man, and so raises it to a higher power, and endows it it with a finer force, and a more valid stability, and a deeper significance. And out of this exaltation of marriage there rises a new fabric, a new wonder —the Christian home, with its exquisite ideal of firm and beautiful order, in which all the several parts are given their full value, and the man is at once master yet servant, and the wife is endowed with grace out of her very weakness, as the curse of pain that lay on child-bearing is transmuted by the sweet honour that belongs to it, since she who was highly favoured became a maiden mother. And the children are made holy, even as the type from which we kneel to learn how to enter the kingdom of heaven by becoming what they are, whose angels behold the face of their true Father Who is in heaven. So the home is rebuilt in Christ; and out of the home come all the virtues that are the secret of good citizenship, as the little casket of gifts that are treasured in the home opens out to fill with its sweet odour the larger home in which all men are made brethren, eating of one loaf, drinking of one cup, members of one body, sealed and bonded together by the one Spirit Who witnesses to the Catholic brotherhood in Christ by His one cry from within each several heart to Abba, the one Father. In all this Christ renovates the body, the family, the society. He enters to become the spring of regenerative forces by which this earthly life is beautifully blessed, and enhanced, and uplifted; and we appeal to all this to justify us in saying that society can only be fully stable, intelligible, and true when it is Christian.

And yet there is another picture ahead haunting us, another figure than this gracious Babe-King on Mary's breast, another scene, with such a different message, it would seem. A lone, forlorn servant of God wanders up and down an earth that rejects and despises Him. Here He can find no home, no abiding-place; more homeless than the bird or the fox, He has not even where to lay His head. The world hates Him, and must hate Him to the end, because He is "not of the world." Round Him rises no fair and melodious human life, with its encompassing tenderness and inwoven lovingkindness. Even from His Mother and His brethren He is roughly parted; a stranger and a pilgrim, He flies from foe to foe, at war with all the powers that go to the building of social life. His kingdom is not of this world; He has no interest that ties Him to earth; He bids his followers have no part or lot with it. He lays down rules which seem, at first sight, to make society impossible; He forswears all thought by which treasure on earth can be laid up, or even food be secured—no purse, no scrip, no sword, no spare garment. He bids the rich sell all and follow Him. He suffers Himself to be kept and fed by the sheer charity of a few women. At last, scourged, stripped, unresisting, He hangs, naked and wounded, between earth and heaven, an eternal protest against a world in which such as He have no place, the world which it is His glory and His joy to leave behind, as He passes to the far home at His Father's side, there where His heart is, there where His hopes are laid up, there whither He ensures an entrance to all sufferers of whom this world is not worthy, who have faith to take up His cross and to die His death.

Here is a very familiar dilemma. It is, indeed, identical with the contrast which puzzled the Jew of old, between the royal and the suffering Messiah, so mysteriously interlaced in the prophetic writings. The antithesis appeared to them far too violent to find its complete solution within the compass of a single personality. They imagined that two separate conceptions of the Christ were thrown into competition. Yet the prophets transferred themselves with absolute freedom and elasticity from the one to the other, without suggesting any variance or any breach of unity. How was it that the two lines of treatment could fuse themselves into a single and consistent realization? That was the question; and it is this same question which recurs when men meet our anxious pleadings for the significance of Christ to all the social, and economical, and political problems which afflict us so sorely, with the rebuffing taunt that we ought—if we were faithful to our crucified Master, if we honestly faced the Sermon on the Mount—to have thrown to the winds the social condition in which we find ourselves living, to have come out of it as out of an unclean thing; that we ought to be without house or home, without purse or scrip, without wife or treasure; we ought to be committed, as He, to poverty, to loneliness, to an open warfare with all the public authorities in Church and State, and probably to a tragic and terrible martyrdom.

Now, I am not asking how far these taunts sting by their truth. Which of us can say frankly and confidently against such criticism, "Let the galled jade wince; our withers are unwrung"? Alas! we do wince; these taunts gall us bitterly. Most certainly very, very few of us are in a position to cast them off without a pang of doubt whether we be not far, far below the standard which He set up for us Who said, "If a man would be My disciple, let him take up his cross and follow Me."

But yet we cannot but observe that the taunt goes far back behind the mere personal and moral question whether you and I are loyal to our homeless Lord. It raises the crucial, intellectual question whether our Lord had anything to say to human and civil society or not. Was His whole teaching unearthly, supernatural, spiritual? Was the Cross nothing but a defiance of all this temporal and transitory existence of ours in the flesh? Did it proclaim aloud the worthlessness of human interests?

And if so, are we all totally and ridiculously mistaken in imagining that Christianity is the very nurse of those excellences and virtues which form the finest and surest material for civic and social uses ; or that it has any message at all to give, as to the family, to the State, or to the use of wealth and the meaning of politics ?

Evidently, as soon as we put the question in that shape, we see that something is wrong, that our critics have overshot their mark, if this is what their criticism of us implies. They are forcing the suffering Christ into antagonism with the royal Christ, Who claims the kingdoms of the earth ; the one conception of Him is being used to undermine and deny the other. If what these people say is true, then the lesson of the Cross is inconsistent with what we learn in the home at Bethlehem ; Good Friday is at variance with Epiphany.

Obviously there is some confusion that so divides the Christ. How has it arisen ? Surely from this, that the Cross is viewed by our critics as the culmination of a human life, while to us it is the condescension of a Divine Life. They view the Cross from below; we, from above. If we follow this out, we shall see, I think, that the asceticism preached by Christ from His Cross is radically and vitally different from all other possible forms in which asceticism meets us, and that it is this reading of the Cross which alone brings into harmonious unity the double conception of Christ on which we have touched, as at once the Consummation of humanity and the Eternal Sufferer.

Let us see this radical difference by contrasting with the mind of Christ the temper to which belong the highest forms of human asceticism

One of the most beautiful stories in which the pathos of this fleeting life has ever embodied itself is that of the first conversion of Sakya Mouni, the Buddha. We all know the well-known tale—how the brilliant and noble young prince stopped in his drive as he passed the loathsome sight of a sick man, shaken with ague, parched with fever, and asked, "Shall I ever be like that?" and how, when his attendants assured him that all must suffer sickness, he rode out no more that day. And again he drove, and stopped in his driving at the sight of an old man, toothless, hairless, crippled, silly, tottering, woe-begone, and asked, "Shall I be like that?" and again they told him, "You, too, must grow old;" and he turned, and went home, and drove no more that day. And, yet again, he drove out and passed a dead body, bare, ugly, rigid, corrupt, and asked, "Shall I be like that?" and they told him again, "You and all must die;" and he turned, went home, and never drove again. For from that hour his heart was set on abandoning all that was glorious and all that was dear—palace and princedom, wife and children; he set out alone to attain wisdom, to become Buddha, to discover and preach the secret of Nirvana.

Here is an ascetic ideal which very superficial people, who are caught by the mere accidental resemblance, are apt to liken to the Christian teaching; but on what is this Eastern ideal founded? Whence does it spring? It springs out of a sense of the worthlessness of all that is human, temporal, fleshly. Here on earth is nothing but illusion; all is fleeting, vanishing, hollow; all passes into decay; all miserably dies. Every form of individual existence is delusive; its feelings, desires, passions, appetites, movements—all are vain, empty, deceitful, aimless. The spirit of wisdom cuts itself off from these. It slits all ties that fasten it down within the network of life; it forsakes all, it spurns all, it makes good its escape, it crosses to the other shore; it passes into eternal stillness untouched by desire.

Here is the spring of Eastern asceticism. Let us turn to the highest Western ideal. What has it to say?

There is no scene in all ancient literature that, for pathos, and beauty, and depth, surpasses the immortal dialogue in which Plato portrays the last hours of his heroic and martyred master. Who can read it without tears? Who that has read it can ever forget it? Here, indeed, we come far nearer to the spirit and tone of Christ, than in the desperate and ghastly pessimism of the Buddha. "I remember," says Phædo, as he tells how Socrates looked and spoke at that final farewell—"I remember the strange feeling that came over me at being with him, for I could hardly believe that I was present at the death of a friend; and I could not pity him; his mien and his language were so noble and fearless in the hour of death that to me he appeared blessed. I thought that in going to the other world he could not be without a Divine call, and that he would be happy, if any man ever was, when he arrived there." How exquisite the Hellenic sanity, the sweet reasonableness of tone, by the side of the passionate Indian nihilism! And of what did Socrates speak? "The wise man," he is saying, "is ever pursuing death, and longing to die, for he is entirely concerned with the soul, and he would like to be altogether quit of the body. The philosopher dishonours his body; his soul runs away from the body and desires to be alone and by herself. For that body is a source of endless trouble; it fills us full of loves, and lusts, and fears, and fancies, and every sort of folly. Whence come wars and factions? Whence, but from the body? The body introduces turmoil and confusion, and hinders us from seeing the truth. Therefore there is no real knowledge possible for us until after death, when God is pleased to release us; and then the foolishness of the body will be cleared away, and we shall be pure, and shall know of ourselves the clear light everywhere, and this is surely the light of truth." Ah! do not the noble words in their exalted simplicity rebuke our laggard, carnal, coward lives? And yet, we must ask again, whence does their force spring? From what root does their sap run? It springs out of the abasement of the human elements, out of the contempt of the higher and willing spirit for the weak and lower flesh. This fair Platonic flower is rooted in bitterness--the bitterness of a disruption, of a life-long quarrel. The mind, assured of its own lofty ambitions, spurns its humbler companion, the body. It frets at the confusions, the turmoils, the appetites, the desires, the motives of the lower self, which cramp its aims and interrupt its studies; it kicks against the pricks of earthly life. This poor humanity of ours, mixed, wayward, wilful, impulsive, passionate, sorrowing and emotional, weeping and laughing, wounded, hurt, dying—all this the wise man cannot make anything of, cannot use, cannot interpret. He asks only to be quit of it. He is at his best when he is farthest off it. He prays for his ultimate and happy release from the tiresome and unintelligible burden. This must be the temper of all high human asceticism that has for its martyrs the heroes of intellect and reason. The magnificence of their martyrdom lies in the revealed supremacy of spirit, as it spurns the ground and flies upward, as it breaks itself against the bars of its carnal cage. The bodily, the human, the emotional, the imperfect —these are flung away, that the spirit may mount. Death is the secret. In death the true manhood makes good its escape.

Now, the Christian asceticism contradicts all this flatly. Its movement is exactly in the opposite direction. It starts from above. The life of the Lord is not a movement of the human spirit upward, attaining its release at death, but a descent of the Divine Spirit downwards, to inhabit, and possess, and secure for its own our frail and fleshly nature. "The Word became flesh, and dwelt among us." The root of our revelation lies in the dignity, the work, the honour, that is brought in upon the flesh of man. It becomes the assured temple of the Word; it receives into itself the glory of God. And all that we have been saying in the last two Sermons fills this out. The Incarnation of Christ is the measure of God's respect for human nature. He places His Son under its limitations, and so recognizes, justifies, eternalizes them. He devotes Himself to saving, illuminating, redeeming it; and this, out of His supreme love for it, which forbids Him to leave it to its sins, or to slay it for its guilt, or to desert it in its shame. God so loves it—loves the human, loves the body, loves the earth—that He sent His only Son to win it again into glory; and so loving it as His child, He takes it as it stands, in its natural earthly condition, just as history had made it, with all its poverties, bruises, diseases, infirmities, with all its blindness, hardness, frailty. All of this He takes into Himself. He will share it all; none of it shall be despised or spurned. Here is the motive, the spirit of Christ's suffering, Christ's asceticism, Christ's Cross. It exhibits, not the pride of the human spirit over against the infirm flesh, but the pity of Divine Spirit for the broken and bruised flesh. It is a display, not of the worthlessness of human life, but of its high and immeasurable worth. The Agony and the Passion of Christ embody the price at which God considers it worth while to redeem the flesh of man. There is His estimate of the value of humanity. God, the Blessed Father, will send His Son to endure even that, if only by so enduring He may recover the body out of sin into salvation. It is all a tribute to the Divine attachment to man, its own creation; it is all a witness to the dignity of that for which the Son of God is content to die. As we stand under that awful Cross and look up at the blood-stained brow, at the pierced side, at the torn limbs, at the closed eyes, at the parched lips ; as we listen to the last dread cry ; it is no martyr we behold, proclaiming the deathless dominance of the Spirit over the weak and wretched human nature, upon which He so bravely triumphs, and from which He so gloriously escapes. The message is just the reverse. It meets us with the challenge : "Look! What is this human nature which you so lightly despise, but to which God, Who created it, clings with such desperate love? How is it that the Divine Spirit puts out such terrible earnestness, spends such tremendous pains, to rescue that earthly, human, fleshly life of yours, which you so proudly condemn as the lower and the baser element? Ask yourselves, what can be the wonder of its dignity, of its possibilities, of its preciousness, of its promise?" "O Lord God," we answer, "what, indeed, is man, that Thou art thus mindful of him? and the Son of man, that Thou so visitest him?"

Two points we may notice as following from this. First, we see how radical is the loss of those who stop short with the conception of Jesus Christ as one among the noble martyrs for the victory of spiritual over fleshly truth. No doubt we may make our approach to the Cross from that side. Jesus Christ did indeed fulfil the martyr ideal; He died on behalf of His sheep; He draws men to His uplifted Cross by the fascination of an heroic sacrifice for truth. His martyrdom forms one of the doorways through which men can pass in, and draw near; and God forbid that we should bar any way by which souls can gain access to grace. Only for men to stop short there, to be caught and imprisoned within that conception of Him, is to miss all that gives to the Cross its peculiar significance, to miss all that gives its special and unique colour to the Christian ascetic temper. That temper takes all its colour, and tone, and character from its belief that the Cross is not the apotheosis of an heroic human spirit, but the pledge of the compassion and love of an Incarnate Son for the human flesh which He has, at such a cost, set Himself to redeem. Its message is, not "through suffering and death lies the escape of the spirit from the burden of the body;" but "through suffering and death lies the road by which the body can become again the purged and purified vessel of Divine glory."

Every one can understand the immense practical difference which that reversal of motive and purpose will effect. Yet all that practical result turns on the dogmatic conception that we have formed of Christ's Person. So inherently dogmatic is Christian practice, so intensely practical is Christian dogma!

And then, again, under this conception of the Christ the problem with which we started solves itself; the royal and the suffering Christ fall together, and become one consistent whole. The suffering of the crucified Christ is the uttermost tribute which the royal Christ pays to the value He sets on the flesh which He has assumed. By assuming it He proclaimed Himself its Lord.

He made evident His estimate of it ; and then, by clinging to it, even at the cost of all that it involved, even at the price of blood, He carried the proof yet further of how dearly and deeply He valued and loved it. The condescension which began in His descending from heaven into the flesh of man completes itself, culminates, in the humiliation to which He submits when He not only emptied Himself of His Godhead, but suffered and died in the fashion of a slave. It is to rescue human nature that He comes to inhabit it ; it is to rescue human nature that He dies in it. All is consistent, all hangs together. There is no divergence between the two aspects, and therefore, to S. John, the Cross on Calvary is the highest display of that glory which shone out in Epiphany. "Now," at that supreme hour of agony on the night of the betrayal—"now is the Son of man glorified, and God is glorified in Him. Now, O Father, glorify Thy Son." The Cross is the final act of that same revelation which began when "the Word took flesh, and dwelt among us, and we saw His glory, the glory as of the only begotten of the Father." The dignity, the honour, the beauty, the preciousness, the sanctity of the flesh, of human nature, of our bodies—that is the surprising Gospel that comes to us from the bodily Passion of the Son of God.

There is indeed a call to the ascetic life, that goes out to every single one among us, from Him Who wandered through our earth, a houseless, homeless pilgrim; from Him Who laid His blessing on those that hunger and mourn and weep; from Him Who was "despised and rejected, the Man of sorrows, acquainted with grief;" from Him Who gave His back to the smiters, and His face to them that plucked off the hair. Yes, there is a call, sharp, clear, decisive. And we, we all, are woefully, miserably far below that call. We hardly dare recall it, or speak of it, in our shame—we who have not once, of our own will, felt the sting of one stripe from the scourge of Christ; we who have never, except under the sheer compulsion of nature, surrendered any pleasure or endured any privation. God grant that nothing said here may relieve our consciences, or put us at our ease, or confirm us in our indolent comfort. No, rather let what is said help to remove out of our way any hindering suspicion which holds us back from taking up the severer discipline of the Cross, any suspicion that we should be dishonouring or despising our human nature by a course of voluntary self-denial, by free sacrifice of pleasure and of ease. "Surely you ought not to go against what is natural and human?" people plead, when we propose anything with a slight flavour of austerity about it; and we feel bothered, perhaps, and puzzled, and do not quite know whether they are not right. Yet surely we might laugh outright at there being anything dishonouring to human nature, to our bodily self, that could ever be sanctioned by the creed which proclaims as its gospel the Divine sanctity of human nature, the glory with which the Word of God has filled the flesh. The discipline, the suffering, the sorrow, which the Cross of Christ calls upon us to lay upon ourselves, and to endure upon earth—what are they? They are the pledges of God's union with our suffering humanity, the witnesses and seals of Christ's perfect sympathy with our flesh and blood, the sacraments of His fellowship with us. And as we thus pass under them, as their shadow darkens over us (which it is bound to do here in the heart of a suffering world), we need not be depressed, morose, inhuman; nothing grim, or black, or fierce need darken our kindliness of nature; for in these trials, and through them, we receive in our souls the kiss of the Man of sorrows, of the Prince of peace. Very near He comes as pain and grief increase; very tender, very gracious, He shows Himself as the blows fall. "See, how I must have loved you," He keeps on whispering, "for even what you now feel so sorely, even that I endured for love of you." What dignity, what glory, lies in this discovery, through experience, of the reality of our brotherhood with Christ! Oh, blessed indeed if we learn to mourn, to hunger, to be persecuted, if so also we learn the unfathomable depths of the compassion of Him Who abhorred nothing which could identify Him with our mortality, and make Him wholly our own!

THE NATURE OF THE FLESH.

"Hereby know ye the Spirit of God: Every spirit that confesseth that Jesus Christ is come in the flesh is of God."—1 JOHN iv. 2.

"THE Word became flesh." No one who pronounces his faith in these words can ever suppose for a moment that there is anything radically and inherently base in the flesh, in human nature. For evidently there is no hint of any alteration in the human character of the flesh to make it fit for God to inhabit. It is our flesh that He became, our nature that He assumed. "Because we, the children, were flesh and blood," therefore He, too, "took of the same," that He might become in everything our very brother, our very own. He took it as He found it, as our own history had made it; with all the burden that sin had laid upon it, with all the woe that sin had worked within it, yet without the sin that caused it. "Without sin," and yet it remained "our flesh." This in itself is a proclamation that sin has no necessary part or lot in the flesh. The Word, indeed, Who assumed it, restored to it its fulness, its reality of being; He brought it back into its true image, its perfect type, its substantial verity. Far from limiting or destroying the nature of flesh by taking it, rather He then re-created it into its rightful character. Flesh became flesh indeed, through the Word Who entered it. It became all that it was meant to be. Its powers were enhanced, its capacities were carried further. It was never so human as when God took it, and therefore never so human, never so fully itself, as when it was made sinless. Far from evil being its true law, its natural inclination, its normal proclivity, its richest freedom, the flesh is spoilt, is poisoned by sin; it corrupts, it falls to pieces, it dies by sinning. It recovers itself in escaping from out of the baneful breath of lust into the pure light and sweet air of holiness. It proves itself to be inherently good, by its natural and spontaneous return to health under the influence of a Divine Indweller. This radical goodness of human nature, in its essential construction, lies at the very root of all the belief in the Incarnation. The suspicion that so often haunts men's minds, lest our flesh should be less itself, should lose something of its humanity by becoming sinless, is a survival in our midst of some antiquated dualism, which the Christian faith exploded and over-mastered fifteen hundred years ago, in the great theology of the fourth century, in the long struggle to cast out and repel all the varied transformations of Platonism and Gnosticism. Once for all, the Church declared then that it was our very flesh which the Word became, very man that Christ was made; and this was obviously impossible, if there was any taint of evil in the verity of our full manhood after the flesh.

But how, then, no doubt many are asking themselves—how, then, of the strong language so proverbial in the Epistles of S. Paul, in which the flesh is set violently and antithetically over against the spirit, language which certainly appears to echo all the worst abuse which the asceticism of ancient philosophy heaped upon the flesh — the flesh which seemed to them the very seat of sin, the very nest of swarming passions, ugly, foul, contemptible? Surely S. Paul justifies all this abuse and scorn when he tells us that "the flesh lusteth against the spirit;" that "the carnal mind is at enmity with God;" that "they that are in the flesh cannot please God."

Now, in estimating this language, we can start with the previous certainty that it is quite impossible that S. Paul should be meaning the same thing as those ascetics who held that the flesh contained in its very nature an evil principle radically antagonistic to the good. For most undoubtedly he had believed from his very childhood, and accepted to the very last hour of his life, the first chapter of Genesis, which declares with unwavering consistency the absolute goodness of the entire creation in its original construction, animal as well as human, bodily as much as spiritual. Upon all that was created went out the approving benediction of God: "God saw all that He had made, and, behold, it was very good." This was S. Paul's creed, and this denied explicitly and emphatically the natural wickedness of the flesh and the dualism of the philosophers. And on to the top of his first faith, S. Paul, as we know with certainty, added belief in the Incarnation, in the descent of God into the flesh of man to justify, approve, sanctify it, out of love for it, to manifest the Godhead in it, to make it the wonder of angels, the consummation of humanity, knitting all human fragments up into the unity of Christ's flesh. This he held with his whole soul; and, so holding, it is absolutely inconceivable that he could have believed the flesh to be inherently and essentially corrupt.

What, then, did he mean? For certainly, through some reason or another, out of some accident, or event, or process, the flesh had, according to him, become the focus, the seat, the scene, the fortress, the theatre, the symbol, the expression, the evidence of all that was bad, base, and godless. How had this come about?

S. Paul himself tells us. He sketches the story, the process, by which this character had accrued to the flesh; and in sketching it he shows with positive clearness that he traced the spring and origin of sin, not to the flesh, but to the spirit, to the will of man. Let us follow S. Paul's summary of this process in the first chapter of the Epistle to the Romans.

How did man's unrighteousness begin?

"When they knew God, they glorified Him not as God." The starting-point of sin is not to be found below, beneath, in some dark swarm of animal passions, climbing up in hideous invasion to the pure heights where the spirit looks out with eyes that search for God. Wholly the contrary; the starting-point is above, in those very heights, at the topmost crown of the moral and intelligent self. Man's highest spiritual office, in which he is at his farthest remove from the animal, is to recognize and glorify God, as He eternally displays Himself to man's contemplation through the beauty and order of visible nature. Here is his special gift, his loftiest prerogative; and it is here, at this point, that he first fails. The vision was clear enough; "the invisible things" of God, His eternal power and Divinity, were clearly to be seen, "being understood by the things that are made." "That which may be known of God was manifest; God showed it to them." Faculties to know God, the evidence for the knowledge, the power to exercise the faculties—all were theirs. And such a vision of God was morally bound to kindle the highest spiritual joy; and such joy would break out in praise, thanks, adoration. But men held off, checked the free outcome. The glow chilled, the outflowing current was blocked. They saw, but they would not rejoice in what they saw. They saw, and to see was to love; but they obstructed the love. The spirit in them that should go out in glorious greetings of a Father

Who made all things good, and did all things well, this spirit perverted itself, shut itself up in hard and cold silence. "When they knew God, they glorified Him not as God, neither were thankful." So came the rift in the lute. Alas for the splendour of that early music of God's dawn, when the morning stars sang together, and all the sons of God shouted for joy! It was with those glad angels that man was called to lift up his voice, under the feet of those who for ever were crying, "Blessing, and honour, and glory, and power, to Him that sitteth upon the throne; for He hath created all things, and for His honour they are and were made." But men held aloof from that sweet singing. This was their sin, "They glorified Him not as God, neither were thankful."

And it could not stop there. The seed is sown. First, the negative—they refuse God the praise; then the positive—the organs that were not exercised in thanksgiving fell into the mischief of idleness. They "became vain in their imaginations." The "imagination," with its reasonings, with its intellectual keenness, with all the brilliant dialectic of the brain, which could, under the Divine Spirit, have searched the deep things of God—this goes off at a tangent; it takes wrong roads; it blunders into specious mistakes; it pursues aimless arguments; it is tangled in clever sophistries; it loses its logical veracity; it reaches no solid and real conclusions; it spends its efforts on vacancy; it is become hollow, empty, vain. They " become vain in their imaginations."

And then "their foolish heart was darkened." The very faculty of reasoning, the heart, lost its capacity, became spoilt, damaged, corrupt, because they had failed to love, to rejoice in what they saw. Therefore now they fail to see; a cloud spreads itself, a dulness of intuition, a stupidity. No alertness, no clear-sightedness; the foolish heart is darkened. Instead of being "wise, they become fools." The sin in the will, which withheld love, stupefies the intellect, lands it in absurdities. We cannot reason aright without loving. A man without love is a stupid man;

he is like an owl in the daylight. So man, through lack of love for God, is losing his power to know God—he " becomes a fool."

And now the folly of the heart spreads downward, the evil descends to a lower stage. First, the folly of the heart shows itself positively in the form of idolatry. The lack of true knowledge about God issues in positive wrong knowledge. Lack of true praise, true adoration, issues in false praise, false adoration. The stupidity of the mind makes man mistake the creature for the Creator. The cloud obscures the lines which divide; the darkened heart cannot hold fast distinctions. All is blurred, blotted, confused. Man fumbles with his subject; he cannot discern between God and Nature. Nature, the visible, the created, looms up before his blinded eyes in immense and gathering grandeur; it occupies his vision; he loses sense of its limits and horizons. The glory that should be God's own prerogative implicates itself with the things on which it is shed; it seems to his duller eyes to be theirs—their own. He gives to them the awe, the fear, the power, which God, through them, rouses in him. Here is the mistake. God's voice speaks to him through the thunder; and man deems that it is the thunder which speaks, and, lo! he crouches and trembles under the mere vapours of a storm-cloud. God's splendour glows through the sunlight; and man bows low before the sun, and offers the child of his body to a blind, hot stone rolling through heaven. God's versatility, God's glory of beauty, pours itself over bird and beast and creeping thing; and man makes the beast his god and worships the creeping thing. The dismal, dreadful blunder, the horrible stupidity of the dark heart, and the vain imagination! Man "changed the truth of God into a lie, and worshipped and served the creature more than the Creator," Who yet, indeed, cannot be dragged down—blessed be His Name!—by such infamous confusion, but sits on high, grave, and pure, and true, whatever man does to degrade and defile Him. Yea, says S. Paul, God, "Who is blessed for ever. Amen."

And now comes the last sad stage. It is at the end, not at the beginning, that we find that sin sinks to the lowest layers, down to that, in man, which we associate so intimately with evil —to the flesh, the appetites, the passions. It comes about as the issue of stupid idolatry, which was due to the darkening of the intellect, which, again, followed on the perversion of spiritual love. All this confusion, this intellectual chaos, this distorted imagination, this misguided will, this erring, wayward, silly sophistry, all this spiritual rebellion against God, drops down, to reappear in the flesh as a tumult, a mob, a disorder, of the desires. The disturbance above creates, as its natural result, the disturbance below. All the sweet seemliness of harmonious order in the emotions breaks up, disappears. There is revolt, violence, extravagance, excess, blindness, ignorance, distraction. Nothing knows its place or office any more. Anarchy shatters the fabric of social affections; they no longer make for unity, no longer knit men together in enduring bonds.

They wander loose and distraught, working mischief, shame, division, hate. The flesh seethes in a wild ferment of disordered and corrupted appetites; and all this disorder is but a symbol, an image, a copy of the sin committed in the secret home of the will. It is its normal and inevitable effect, and that effect God sanctions; it fulfils God's own laws in which man was created. "God gave them up to uncleanness through the lusts of their own hearts." It could not but happen, and God approved the necessity. Because "they changed the truth of God into a lie," therefore "God gave them up unto vile affections." He suffered the natural result to follow, unhindered by Him. "Even as they did not like to retain God in their knowledge, God gave them over to a reprobate mind, to do those things which are not convenient." And so the works of the flesh revealed themselves in their full force, in their fatal savagery. They became "filled with all unrighteousness, fornication, wickedness, . . . maliciousness; full of envy, murder, debate, deceit, malignity; . . . haters of God, . . . without understanding, . . . without natural affection, implacable, unmerciful."

Now, there is S. Paul's account of the origin of the sins of the flesh; and Christian doctrine has never for a moment wavered in its loyalty to this description. Always it has protested with vigour against the Manichæism which made evil to be a quality, a natural attribute, of a lower and fleshly element in man. Always it has declared with emphasis that there is no such thing known to it as an evil nature; there is nothing existent whose true property it is to be evil. All that is in the highest sense natural must be good, for God created nature. Christianity has only one account to give of sin—that it is a perversion of good, a distortion of nature, an unnatural corruption.

Ah! but "the natural man," you will say, "the natural man is at enmity with God." Do not let that expression confuse us for an instant. The "natural man" is sinful because man's nature is supernatural. It is unnatural, it is against the real laws of his nature, for him to be merely natural. If man drops to the level of his lower self, to the level of that which he has in common with creatures lower than he; if he confines himself to the limited horizons of the animal; if he in that sense hugs the natural and refuses to look beyond and rise above it, then he sins not only against his higher self—his mind, imagination, spirit—but he sins against his very lower self, within whose bounds he shuts himself in. He sins against his nature, against his flesh; for that flesh counted on the lift it was to receive through the soaring spirit. That body was made so as to receive its transfiguration through the light that should stream down into it out of the illuminated world with which its intellect, and its will, and its love were to bring it in contact. Its nature was ready to respond to that replenishing, to that upward draw. And now it has missed its aim, it has lost its development. It is the flesh which so desperately feels the damage and realizes the loss; and all its consequent trouble and turmoil is but the accusing cry which it utters against the false and disloyal spirit which, by professing to be natural, has wrecked its nature—by sinking to the lower level of the flesh, has irretrievably thwarted the tendencies and capacities of the flesh. Man, in becoming natural, sins against his nature; and it is the higher and not the lower elements in man which are guilty of this sinful lapse, for it is they who are responsible for the failure of the natural to rise, as it was bound to do, up into the supernatural. No; our position is not confused—it is emphasized—by the phrase which makes "the natural man" the expression of disgrace and degradation. Christian theology knows but of one source from whence sin can spring— "an evil will." Evil has a spiritual source ; and such evil can never be a natural quality, but always a distorted good; for that will which makes sin exist, was certainly so created as to adore God. S. Augustine himself, the great exponent of the evil in the natural man, is also the master exponent of this conception of sin.

But now we can see easily enough why, when once the sin has taken place, "the flesh," "the natural man," became the normal expression by which the sinful condition so produced can be described. Man's sin is, as we have said, that he through disloyalty of spiritual desire has become merely fleshly, merely natural; he has become carnal. The flesh, in its disorganization, in its demoralization, in its corruption, makes evident and makes permanent the horrid lapse of faith. Not only are its functions all thrown into tumult and faction, but worse. It has now admitted within its confined circle those finer powers which were intended for higher and vaster occupations. They have deserted their post, their watch-tower, where they were to be ever beholding and worshipping the face of Him Who created the body as well as the spirit. Down they have dropped, and now they are discharging their magnificent forces into the narrow channels laid open to them in the flesh. The imagination, which ought to be reviewing the beauty of God's har-

monious work, is now lending horrible power to
the passions, as it expands their range and kindles
their hot blood by its swift fancies, and eager
curiosities, and far-reaching suggestions. It feeds
them with conceits ; it prompts them with pictures ;
it maddens them with poisonous art. And the
intellect, which ought to be unravelling and reveal-
ing the whole counsel of God, is giving eyes to the
appetites, and is creating new and growing hungers
before unknown to the quiet and innocent flesh.
Ever it goes wider afield, catering with its rapid
and audacious skill for the desires which it has filled
with clamorous greeds. It schemes ever for more ;
its ambition is insatiable ; it is never fatigued in
contriving new sensual delights. And hither and
thither, making use both of imagination and of
intellect, pushes and presses the rebel will. It has
forgotten its great office of gathering up the entire
man into a single and whole offering, a willing
Eucharist, held high by it before the altar of
God, blameless and unspotted. It is now buried
within the natural man, bent on self-gratification,

through the pleasures, through the senses, through the feelings. Those feelings, those senses, that were meant to move in sweet obedience to man's upward spiritual growth, are now impregnated with all the heat and fever of the will. It inserts itself within them, and works like leaven, and seeks in them its own fulfilment, and pushes them forward into more extravagant claims, and uses every faculty that man possesses to enlarge and intensify the pride with which it asserts man's right to enjoy. Whatever of possible satisfaction the imagination can picture, or the intellect can descry, over the broad earth, that the will in the man spreads itself to reach and have.

Here is, indeed, the carnal mind which is at enmity with God, the mind which has for its field, for its object, for its matter, the needs of the flesh. We men dare to call those passions "animal," as if any animal possessed those extravagant desires, or exhibited this tumult of excess. Nay; it is because these passions are ours, are human, that they become endowed with such fearful exuberance.

And it is the reason and the will of man which dower them with this fatal wealth; and "out of the flesh" which they have thus demoralized proceed all the works of the flesh—adultery, fornication, lasciviousness, uncleanness, idolatry. And, just because an unnatural strength has been lent to the passions, therefore they never can attain the satisfaction which they seek, and fall back in sickly lassitude from an ever-failing hope, and loathe their own life, and hate the world which so deceives them, and become ever more full of cruelty, and malice, and malignity, and so give birth to those other works of the flesh—hatred, variance, emulations, strife, sedition, heresies, envyings, murders, drunkenness, and such like.

How terribly we ourselves may know this history of sin, this horror of the flesh! We hate, we accuse the flesh, because it is in the flesh that sin displays its final and inevitable and enduring results. The flesh is the scene on which it makes itself evident, and asserts the dominion it has won. But the sin itself is always in the will, in the secret inward man. There it is that we commit rebellion, that we turn perverse. And no doubt this inner sin seems to us but a slight, passing, transitory lapse a momentary indulgence in a loose desire an idle and indolent slip in falsehood, a flash of nasty and cruel spite, that came and went. And we were very sorry for it; and we hastily resolved to avoid so falling again; and then we forgot it. It was but a little thing, and it is done and over now, and we have regretted it. All is right; nothing remains. It was hidden away in the secret man, and surely it is gone as soon as it has been passed by and forgotten. Very lightly we treat it; very easily we fancy it can all be put away. Alas! it may have gone, but it has left disorder behind it; and the flesh, the lower man, bears the traces of that disorder. Into it the deposit of sin has been made; down through it the germ works like poison. That flying curiosity has set moving the swarm of appetites; that passing malice has tickled the passions that make for hate. A strange and dreadful disturbance wakes up; at some hour when we are not expectant or aware, it breaks out over us like a disease. We are startled; we shrink back; we protest; we did not believe we were capable of such wicked wishes. It is horrible, and we call it bad names. We say, " It is not us ; we are purer, better, holier than this ; it is our animal passions that insult and defile us." No, no! Let us at least be honest; let us know ourselves. This horror of ourselves, which is our ruin if we pride ourselves on it, or content ourselves with it, may be our salvation if we recognize in it our own inner guilt, which in its invisible stealth escapes our judgment, but which, in and through the visible evidence of the flesh, discloses, even to *our* eyes, its deformity, its vileness, its permanence, its seriousness, its peril. So, as we learn how real and definite a matter sin is, we may learn also how equally real and definite must be the pains we take to undo and remove its effects.

Lastly, one short word of warning. We see

the dangers of an evil we may think lightly of—spiritual sloth, spiritual indolence. The terrible power which is given to the passions comes to them through our failure to keep in exercise the higher faculties, imagination, intellect, will, on their true object, the vision and glory of God. Through that failure these powers descend, sink, grow confused, obscured; they seek fulfilment in false ways; they turn their attention upon the flesh; they pour into its channels their abundance and heat; they influence it; they lend it monstrous and unnatural strength. The desires acquire a horrid violence as they feel pushing and alive within them the full force of a deteriorated intellect, a perverted imagination, a prostituted will. These, that should be the priests of the pure manhood in us, lifting on high holy hands to sanctify and offer, are now reckless and demoralized even as priests who have been unfrocked and degraded. They cast loose their shame; they lose all the sense of scruple. And all this may come about through leaving these highest gifts unused, leaving them to vacant, wayward, undisciplined idleness. Believe me, it is not with impunity that we so idle. Intellect, imagination, will—these must find food, occupation, exercise, somewhere or somehow. If we do nothing for their right employment, they will find it for themselves elsewhere; they will animate the flesh until it has power, like a wild beast, to turn and tear us, who have allowed it to develop into such unlooked-for size and strength. Then, when we feel its claws in us, it will be too late for us to cry out.

God grant us grace now betimes to prevent the evil growth, to cut off its supplies, to drag up our mind and heart to their true office, to discipline and train them in the exercise of their true joy in God. This is our one office; and this, if we choose, we are enabled to do in the Name of Him the Word, Who for our sakes was made flesh, and of His great pity, dwelt among us.

www.ingramcontent.com/pod-product-compliance
Lightning Source LLC
Chambersburg PA
CBHW032047230426
43672CB00009B/1496